CommonSense InvestSense:

The Power of the Informed Investor

James Watkins

Copyright © 2018 James W. Watkins, III. All rights reserved.

No part of this book may be reproduced, stored in a retrieval system, or transmitted in any form or by any means, electronic, mechanical photocopying recording, or otherwise without prior written permission.

Limits of Liability/Disclaimer of Warranty: This book is intended to offer only general information with respect to the subject matter covered. While the publisher and the author have used their best efforts in preparing this book, they make no representations or warranties with respect to the accuracy or completeness of the contents of this book and specifically disclaim any implied warranties of merchantability or fitness for a particular purpose. The advice and strategies herein may not be suitable for your situation. You should consult with a professional where specific expert assistance is required. Publication of this book neither provides, nor is intended to provide, any legal, financial, tax, or accounting advice, services or other professional services. Neither the publisher nor author shall be liable for any loss or profit or any other commercial damages, including but not limited to special, incidental, consequential, or other damages.

Table of Contents

1.	Why Didn't They Tell Me That?	1
2.	Everyone Is <u>Not</u> Losing Money: Investment Myths and the Losses They Create	4
3.	Why Should I Do That?	13
4.	Evaluating a Mutual Fund's Costs and Fees	18
5.	Evaluating a Mutual Fund's Returns	20
6.	Asset Allocation and Market Timing	25
7.	Putting It All Together: The Active Management Value Ratio™ 3.0	31
8.	Investment "Games"	38
9.	Annuities: Reading Between the Marketing Lines	43
10.	Proactive Wealth Preservation: Avoiding the "Tricks of the Trade"	59
11.	The REAL Secret to Successful Investing	63
	Notes	66
	About the Author	70

Chapter One
Why Didn't They Tell Me That?

"Your account is a brokerage account and not an advisory account. Our interests may not always be the same as yours. Please ask us questions to make sure you understand your rights and our obligations to you, including the extent of our obligations to disclose conflicts of interest and to act in your best interest. We are paid both by you and, sometimes, by people who compensate us based on what you buy. Therefore, our profits and our salesperson's compensation, may vary by product and over time."

The foregoing disclosure was part of a rule enacted by the Securities and Exchange Commission ("SEC") in an effort to address an ongoing dispute about the disparity of standards between stockbrokers and investment advisers. The Financial Planning Association sued the SEC over the disparity and won, with the court striking down the rule and requiring that stockbrokers charging fees for investment advice register as an investment adviser.

The SEC revoked the rule, so investors do not currently receive the warning That is the whole purpose of this book. I believe that all investors should be treated fairly. There is a well-known saying in the investment industry, "putting lipstick on a pig." That describes when a stockbroker or other product salesman tries to stress the "alleged" benefits of an investment product or investment strategy while concealing the unfavorable aspects of the product or strategy. My goal in writing this book is to teach you how to spot the "pigs" and "lipstick" in order to better manage your investment accounts and retirement accounts.

- A study by Schwab Institutional found that 75 percent of investor portfolios were unsuitable for investors given their financial situation and goals.[1] Based upon my personal experience, I would put that number closer to 90 percent or higher based on issues involving inadequate, or "pseudo," diversification;

- A recent study by CEG Worldwide concluded that over 94 percent of those holding themselves out as wealth managers were more product salesman than wealth manager[2];
- Investment fraud is the number crime against the elderly, affecting an estimated 7.3 million older Americans, or one out of every five senior citizens[3]. Since that number only counts the instances of fraud actually reported, the number of victims is undoubtedly higher.

Most people are familiar with the saying, "knowledge is power." Thomas Jefferson reportedly went even further, saying that "knowledge is power, knowledge is protection, knowledge is happiness." Nowhere is that truer than in connection with personal finance and investing. Knowledge provides you with the power to protect your financial security, which in turn promotes you personal happiness.

Nothing gives me more pleasure than teaching someone how to spot investment scams and being able to protect their financial security. I routinely get calls from pension plans, trusts and investors asking me to perform a forensic audit to make sure that their investment accounts are properly structured and fundamentally sound. Sadly, in many cases they are not.

I have been teaching individuals and institutions the "tricks of the trade" in investing for a couple of years. As I explain some of the "tricks" that cost people to lose money investing, the most frequent question is always something along the lines of "why didn't they tell me that?" My usual answer is usually "because if they had told you the whole truth, you would never have bought what they were trying to sell you."

I always tell groups that I am not going to ask them if they have been a victim of any of these "tricks"/investment scams. I tell them they are free to talk to me after the class if they wish. As we go through my system, their faces quickly let me know that they have been victims of some of the more common abusive investment marketing strategies. As you go through this book, how many times you find yourself asking—"why didn't they tell me that?"

InvestSense IQ: Don't confuse investment "brains" with a bull market!

Chapter Two
Everyone Is <u>Not</u> Losing Money:
Investment Myths and the Losses They Create

Financial advisors often explain investment losses with the mantra "it's the economy/market, everyone is losing money." When an investor asks me to perform a fiduciary audit and tells me that that was the explanation given to them for the poor performance of their portfolio, I tell them that statements like that generally reveal that (1)their financial advisor is either intellectually dishonest and cannot be trusted, and/or (2) the advisor does not really understand wealth management, especially portfolio risk management.

The investment industry has created a false sense of security in investors by perpetuating, either intentionally or unintentionally, various investment myths. In many cases, investors have read or heard these myths so many times that they have come to accept these myths as true, without taking the time to actually determine their accuracy. Unfortunately, investors often suffer unnecessary investment losses as a result of their blind acceptance of such myths.

People in the investment industry may react strongly when such accusations are made. However, a review of the last two bear markets, 2000-2002 and 2007-2008, raises a number of legitimate questions regarding the role that popular investment myths and misconceptions played in contributing to the bear market losses suffered by investors. It is worthwhile to consider some of the more popular investment myths and examine how they can negatively impact an investor's returns.

Investment Myths

1. *"It's the market/economy. Everyone is losing money."*

A recent Wall Street Journal article discussed "The Lost Decade" of investing, as the 2007-2008 bear market effectively wiped out the market's gain over the past decade.[4] Volatility can have a significant impact on investment returns. Consequently, consistency of returns and the avoidance of large losses are keys to successful investing.

Too many investors get so caught up with maximizing returns that they fail to consider the importance of preserving their gains through an effective risk management strategy. A popular saying on Wall Street is "don't confuse brains with a bull market." This saying reflects the fact that approximately two-thirds of all investments follow the direction of the prevailing trend of the market. Therefore, it is actually hard <u>not</u> to make money during a secular bull market.

The real key to investment success is how well investors use risk management techniques during bear markets to preserve their wealth. It is for that reason that Charles Ellis points out that the true value of an investment advisor lies more in their ability to manage market risk than in their ability to generate investment returns.[5] Effective investment risk management can range from simple strategies, such as reallocating, replacing and/or rebalancing current assets, to more complex strategies, such as using bear/inverse index funds or options, such as protective puts, to protect an investor's portfolio.

In some cases, other investment myths contribute to a failure to implement appropriate risk management strategies. In other cases, conflicts of interest may prevent the development of an effective risk management plan. Regardless of the reason, a failure to properly manage investment risk needlessly exposes an investor to the risk of significant financial loss.

2. *Stockbrokers, investment advisors and other "financial advisors" are required to always put their clients' interests first and to disclose any actual or potential conflicts of interest.*

Investment advisors, including financial planners, are, by law, fiduciaries. As fiduciaries, they are held to the highest standards in connection with their dealings with the public. Fiduciaries are required to always put their clients' interests first, to disclose any actual or potential conflicts of interest, and only recommend "prudent" investments, the same investments that they would choose for their own portfolios.

Stockbrokers, however, are generally not considered to be fiduciaries. Consequently, they are not required to put their clients' interests first or to disclose all information regarding actual or potential conflicts of interest. While fiduciaries are required to only recommend investments that are in a client's best interests, stockbrokers are only required to recommend investments that are "suitable." Which leads to the obvious question-how can an investment be considered to be in a customer's "best interests" if it is not also considered to be prudent?

The Securities and Exchange Commission (SEC) is currently engaged in a heated debate with their proposed Regulation "Best Interest" (Reg BI), which would supposedly require all stockbrokers providing investment advice to the public to always put a customer's best interests ahead of their own. Meanwhile, the Financial Industry Regulatory Agency (FINRA), one of the two primary agencies, along with the SEC, that regulate stockbrokers, recently stated that their suitability standard and the "best interest" standard are "inextricably intertwined."

The monthly list of enforcement actions on both the Financial Industry Regulatory Agency (FINRA) and the SEC web sites prove that simply enacting rules alone neither ensures that financial advisors will comply with such rules nor guarantees the quality of investment advice an investor receives. While FINRA, the SEC and state regulatory departments audit broker-dealers and investment advisory firms, they have neither the time nor the resources to review each customer account, each recommendation and each transaction made within an account.

In theory, the internal compliance department in each broker-dealer and investment advisory firm should be able to detect and to prevent improper activity by their representatives. Unfortunately, there are simply too many cases where theory and reality produce different results. Bottom line, investors must become more proactive and take greater responsibility for managing both their financial advisors and their financial affairs in order to protect their financial security.

3. *Modern Portfolio Theory's "optimal" investment portfolio is the best investment option for every investor.*

The concept of Modern Portfolio Theory (MPT) and its use in creating the "optimal" investment portfolio was introduced in 1952 by Dr. Harry M. Markowitz. Prior to Dr. Markowitz's work, investment portfolios were usually created by considering only an investment's returns and the variance of such returns. Dr. Markowitz argued that the correlation of returns should also be factored into the investment portfolio construction process.

Many financial advisors use MPT-based commercial software programs to prepare asset allocation and portfolio optimization recommendations for their clients. Clients are usually given various spreadsheets and multi-color charts, along with the advisor's asset allocation/portfolio optimization recommendations for the "optimal" investment portfolio. In truth, the charts, the spreadsheets and the recommendations generally do little more than create a false sense of security for investors and provide recommendations that may be totally inappropriate for the client.

What many investors, and for that matter their financial advisors, do not realize is that Markowitz himself cautioned that the most efficient investment portfolio based on MPT, the "optimal" portfolio, may not be the appropriate choice for every investor. Markowitz pointed out that in designing the proper portfolio for an investor, both an investor's willingness to accept investment risk and their ability to bear such risk must be considered.[6]

Another reason why investors often suffer unnecessary losses as a result of MPT's "optimal" portfolio approach is that the calculation process used by MPT is inherently unstable and easily susceptible to manipulation. MPT uses a process known as means-variance optimization to produce asset allocation recommendations. MVO has an inherent bias toward investments that have high returns and a low level of variance in returns. Slight errors in the input data can result in disproportionately larger errors in the recommendations produced, leading one expert to characterize MPT-based portfolio optimization software programs as "estimation-error maximizers."[7]

Another concern about relying on MPT-based asset allocation recommendations is that the value of such recommendations depends on the reliability of the input data used, the proverbial "garbage in, garbage out" syndrome. Most MPT-based commercial software programs use historical risk and return numbers for their input data, even though "past performance does not guarantee future performance." Markowitz himself preferred that estimates of future returns and variances be used in MVO calculations. However, the difficulty in predicting the future and the potential financial consequences for being wrong on such predictions makes the reliance on such "guesstimates" troubling.

Too often, MPT is simply a means to an end, a quick way to produce a financial plan to justify a fee and/or to market financial products, with little or no consideration given to the inherent value of the plan's recommendations. Once a financial plan has been prepared, an investor should ask the financial advisor who prepared the plan to go back and recalculate the plan's projected risk and return numbers based upon the financial advisor's recommendations or the actual investments sold to the investor.

The overwhelming majority of financial advisors cannot perform such investment specific calculations, as commercial asset allocation/portfolio optimization software programs are generally limited to performing calculations based on broad, generic asset allocation categories. Consequently, many critics of such pseudo-financial planning argue that such plans are nothing more than expensive paper airplane kits.

4. *Asset allocation explains 93.6 percent of the investment returns of an investment portfolio.*

This statement is based on a 1986 paper by Gary P. Brinson, L. Randolph Hood and Gilbert L. Beebower (BHB) entitled "Determinants of Portfolio Performance."[5] BHB studied 91 large pension plans and analyzed the plans' returns based on the plans' allocation among three investment options – stocks, bonds and cash. Based on their study, BHB concluded that investment policy i.e., asset allocation "explained, on average, 93.6 percent of the total *variation* in actual plan returns."[9] (emphasis added).

What investors need to know about the BHB myth is that BHB studied the determinants of the variation of returns, not the determinants of the total returns themselves. Variability of returns is significantly different from total returns, with no absolute correlation between the two.

In retrospect, the BHB findings are not that profound. Historically, stocks are more volatile than bonds and bond are more volatile than cash. Therefore, not surprisingly, the BHB study simply concluded that increasing the percentage of a portfolio's allocation in riskier investments increases the variability of returns, or volatility, of the overall portfolio.

BHB never claimed to have examined the impact of asset allocation on determining actual portfolio returns, let alone claim that asset allocation explains 93.6 percent of a portfolio's actual returns. The investment industry, however, has manipulated the findings of the BHB study and combined it with yet another investment myth to promote perhaps the most devastating investment myth of all.

Subsequent studies have disputed BHB's findings and the exact impact of asset allocation on portfolio management. The important point for investors is that asset allocation is an important aspect of the wealth management process, although just one aspect of the process.

5. *A buy-and-hold approach is the best way to manage one's investments.*

Combine the MPT myth with the BHB myth and you get the 'buy-and-hold" myth. Neither Dr. Markowitz nor Dr. William F. Sharpe, both Nobel laureates for their work in the area of portfolio management, has advocated that a portfolio's allocation mix should always remain static. In fact, Dr. Sharpe has stated that a portfolio's allocation should be flexible in order to adapt to and to benefit from changes in the economy and the markets.[10]

Nevertheless, the investment industry continues to perpetuate the notion that the best investment strategy for investors is a buy-and-hold approach. Investors have heard or read about the buy-and-hold proposition so many times that they just assume that it is true, even though the history of the markets clearly indicates otherwise. While buy-and-hold works during secular bull markets and perhaps for certain specific investments, the buy-and-hold approach completely ignores the cyclical nature of the broad-based markets and the impact of secular bear markets.

Just ask index investors how well a buy-and-hold approach served them during both the 2000-2002 and the 2007-2008 bear markets. Between October 2007 and November 2008, the S&P 500 Index lost 51.9 percent of its value. In order to recover the loss, an investor had to earn a return of approximately 107.9 percent, not factoring in inflation.

Sadly, such losses could have and should have been either avoided altogether or at least mitigated had investors and their advisors heeded the market's warnings. Buy-and-hold advocates generally ignore such "warnings," arguing that such techniques constitute market timing and that market timing does not work. They are absolutely correct insofar as they are referring to classic market timing, which attempts to time short-term swings in the market.

However, the buy-and-hold argument becomes disingenuous when applied to intermediate and long term investing, as it completely ignores the cyclical nature of the broad based market and the value of avoiding significant losses. Responding to changes in the economy and/or in intermediate and long terms trends in the market by acting proactively to prevent significant and unnecessary investment losses is simply intelligent and prudent wealth management, not market timing.

Just before the onset of the 2000-2002 bear market, the price-earnings ratio on the Dow Jones Industrial Average (DJIA) stood at an all-time high of 43, almost twice as high as the DJIA's previous price-earnings ratio high and almost 150 percent above the DJIA's historic average price-earnings ratio of 16-17. As a result of the dot.com craze, people were paying irrational prices for stocks of companies that had never even shown an annual profit. The question was not *if* there would be a bear market, only *when* it would occur.

Buy-and-hold advocates simply chose to ignore such signs, resulting in disastrous and unnecessary investment losses. As Aldous Huxley pointed out, "facts do not cease to exist simply because one chooses to ignore them."

Buy-and-hold advocates also point to tax efficiency as an advantage of their approach to investing. While the tax implications of an investment strategy should always be considered, an investor should remember why they chose to invest in the first place, to make money in pursuit of their financial goals. Investors should never allow the tax "tail" to wag the investment "dog."

Since the defensive measures being considered here would presumably involve intermediate and long term investment holdings, any taxes that would be incurred would be based on the lower capital gains tax rate and not on the higher ordinary income tax rate. Ask investors who suffered losses of 40-50 percent during the 2000-2002 and 2007-2008 bear markets if they would have been willing to pay 15 percent in capital gains tax to preserve the value of their portfolios. That is even truer in tax-deferred accounts such as 401(k), 403(b) and IRA accounts, where changes can be made with no immediate tax implications.

Given the evidence against using a buy-and-hold approach for intermediate and long term investing, one has to wonder why a financial advisor would advocate such a strategy for a client. Many investors may not realize that most actively managed mutual funds pay annual 12b-1 fees to financial advisors for as long as the advisor's customers own their funds. Combine that fact with the fact that all financial advisors are not required to put their customers' interests first, and perhaps the steadfast advocacy of a buy-and-hold approach makes more sense.

6. *Just wait, the market will recover.*

This is not so much a myth as it is an incomplete and misleading statement. Markets generally do recover, but the time spent on recovering from losses is an opportunity cost since an investor must use those recovery returns just to break even from the earlier losses. It took almost six years for the S&P 500 Index to recover the losses it suffered during the 2000-2002 bear market. As mentioned earlier, an S&P 500 Index investor had to earn a return of approximately 107.9%, not factoring in inflation, in order to recover from the S&P 500 Index's 51.9% loss during the 2007-2008 bear market.

Investors who are proactive and take defensive measures in order to protect their wealth get to accumulate more "true" wealth during the market's recovery. Simply put, it's very hard for an investor to get ahead if they have to spend all their time catching up.

The financial losses suffered during the 2000-2002 and 2007-2008 bear markets changed millions of investors' lives. Despite allegations to the contrary, everyone did <u>not</u> lose money during these bear markets, at least not to the extent of the losses in the broad market indexes.

The unprecedented 1982-1999 bull market led many investors to forget the historical pattern of two bullish periods and one bearish period over every three years. By failing to factor in the inevitable bearish periods in the markets, many investors left themselves exposed to the risk of unnecessary financial loss.

Investors who use effective risk management strategies and ignore various investment myths and misconceptions increase their odds of earning acceptable returns in both bull and bear markets. On the other hand, investors who fail to respect the history of the markets and fail to properly manage investment risk should remember any financial losses from the recent bear markets and George Santayana's warning – which "those who do not remember the past are doomed to repeat it."

Chapter Three
Why Should I Do That?

I am a securities/ERISA attorney, a CFP® professional, and an Accredited Wealth Management Professional℠. They are several prestigious designations. However, one of the common mistakes investors make is being intimidated by professional designations that financial advisers have earned, so much so that they just defer to a professional, with many claiming to being too intimidated to ask questions they may have or being afraid of appearing "foolish."

It's your money! Ask any questions you may have. For an investor to have a meaningful and truly beneficial relationship with their financial adviser, they need to feel comfortable enough to ask any question they want to ask the adviser, to understand all the "whys" involved in their financial/investment plan. I have written several posts on my two blogs about the importance of asking "why," and the importance of continuing to ask "why" until you understand the answers you receive and the rationale provided for each answer.

One of my favorite real-life stories about the power of "why" involves a wife who had recently been widowed. She had gone to visit a "financial adviser" about making sure her affairs were in order. Had the widow followed the financial adviser's recommendations, there would have definitely been catastrophic financial and emotional consequences.

Most experienced investment advisers and financial planners will tell you that studies consistently conclude that such "canned" questionnaires have little or no value due to the tendency of investors to overestimate their risk tolerance unless they have actually suffered an actual down, or "bear," market. Ask people who actually endured the bear markets of 2000-2002 and/or 2008 what their risk tolerance is now and if it changed after those bear markets.

The widow's husband had done an excellent job of positioning their portfolio to provide for her after he was gone. As with many couples, he had handled all the couple's financial affairs while he was alive.

That has gradually changed today, as wives are more are involved in a couple's financial affairs.

In filling out the financial adviser's risk tolerance questionnaire, one of the questions asked if the widow needed additional income. Her husband had allocated the portfolio in such a way that it would produce more than enough dividend income to provide for her needs. Not only that, he utilized a popular strategy that rotates dividend payouts so that she received sufficient dividends quarterly.

However, the risk tolerance questionnaire could not know the excellent portfolio plan the husband had devised. Instead, the computer misinterpreted the widow's honest answers to mean that she had no income needs at all. As a result, the computer produced an asset allocation plan that would have totally destroyed the dividend system and re-allocated her entire portfolio in non-dividend producing, overpriced and historically underperforming actively managed equity mutual funds. It would have been total disaster, both financially and emotionally.

This is one of the reasons I am not as big a fan of robo-advisers as some other financial advisers. These robo-advisers have yet to be tested by a true bear market. As a result, we do not yet know if the restricted asset management strategies practiced by many of the robo-advisers will provide the downside wealth preservation and protection needed to avoid significant financial losses.

Another story that stresses the need to ask questions of investment advisers and seek more than one opinion had to do with a family that was devastated by an automobile accident that left two young children orphaned. The family went to our church and I had actually coached the children in t-ball and was close to them. Unfortunately, a dispute arose in the family as to the management of the children's respective trusts set up under their parents' wills.

One of the family members asked me to review the financial recommendations that a financial adviser had prepared. As soon as I looked at the plan, I recognized it as a product of a program that one of my previous employers had used.

In the financial planning/investment industry, there is a term known as "black box planning." This refers to the fact that many financial planners use computer applications to create comprehensive financial plans and/or specialized planning modules covering one or two limited issues. The concern with "black box planning" is that the computer program may be the one actually producing the "plan," without sufficient human input to ensure the overall quality of the advice and the recommendations being provided.

That is exactly what happened in this case. The recommendations may have been technically appropriate and according to the "book." However, the adviser totally failed to consider the practical concerns, such as this was possibly the children's only source of income for at least the early portion of their life.

Therefore, safety of principal and capital preservation had to be the immediate and primary concerns. The adviser's recommendations suggested an asset allocation that was way too heavy in equity-based mutual funds, historically underperforming, actively managed funds loaded with front-end loads and other unnecessary costs and charges.

InvestSense IQ: I'll repeat this mantra several times during this book: Each 1 percent in fees and other costs reduces an investor's end-return by approximately 17 percent over a twenty year period.

My purpose in writing this book was not to bore or confuse your with a discourse in technical analysis or investment theory. While I enjoy a discussion about Ichimoku clouds and Bollinger Bands as much as the next investment nerd, my goal here is to provide investors with a simple, straightforward system that they can use to help them build and preserve their investment portfolios.

Active versus passive portfolio management is a subject of great debate. A common saying is that "you cannot time the stock market." Trying to perfectly time complete movements 100% in or 100% out of the stock market is generally acknowledged to be futile and expensive, both in terms of trading costs and taxes.

At the same time, I am not one of those who believe that every modification in a portfolio's allocations constitutes trying to "time" the stock market. After all, if one accepts the "any reallocation" definition of market timing, then technically rebalancing, a portfolio management strategy widely accepted in investment circles, would constitute "timing."

Another common investment saying is that "trees do not grow to the sky." History has shown us that stock markets are cyclical, alternating between "strong/up,", or "bull" markets, and "weak/down," or "bear," markets. In between "bull" and "bear markets, the stock markets suffer "corrections," relatively small dips in the stock markets of ten percent or less.

One popular risk management technique recommended by many investment advisers is to periodically rebalance your investment portfolio's asset allocation percentages to restore them to their original allocations. The theory is that by constantly maintaining your portfolio's allocations within a certain range, e.g., 5 percent of their original allocations, an investor hopefully avoids suffering significant losses. It takes longer to recover from portfolio losses since there will be less principal in the beginning on which to build/compound.

Loss Suffered	Return Required
10%	11%
20%	25%
30%	43%
40%	67%
50%	100%

One last comment on "market timing." In his classic, "Winning the Loser's Game," investment icon Charles D. Ellis suggests that contrary to public opinion, while most investors chase investment returns, successful investing is actually a *defensive* process,[11] the avoidance of significant losses.

Benjamin Graham is widely considered the "father of modern investing." In his classic book, "The Intelligent Investor," Graham suggests a conservative, defensive portfolio management system that investors can use.[12] Graham suggests that every investor start off with a simple 50%/50% allocation between equities and fixed income. Graham then suggests that an investor can vary their allocations depending on their confidence in the stock market. However, Graham suggests that neither the equity nor the fixed income allocations should never drop below 25 percent. That way an investor always has a presence in the stock market and can fully participate in the market's recovery.

Buy and hold advocates always point out that making changes in an investment portfolio can have adverse tax consequences. That is true in some cases. However as mentioned earlier, investors should never let the "tax tail wag the investment dog." Investors simply need to factor in both the potential tax consequences and the potential investment loss consequences when considering making changes in their investment portfolios. Investors also need to remember that there are generally no immediate tax implications for making changes in tax-deferred accounts like retirement accounts.

Chapter Four
How Do I Evaluate a Mutual Fund's Costs and Fees?

Right now, there is a debate going on within the investment industry regarding the standard of care that stockbrokers and their broker-dealers should be held to when providing investment advice, as opposed to simply selling investment products to the public. Stockbrokers and broker-dealers are generally held to a "suitability," or "just OK is enough" standard. Registered investment advisers and their members, known as "investment advisory representatives," are held to a much more demanding "fiduciary" standard of care which requires them to always put a client's "best interests" first.

Personally, it is hard to imagine a scenario where an investor would prefer "just OK" advice when they could insist on investment advice that is in their "best interests." "Best" versus "just OK." The Securities and Exchange Commission has promised to make a final decision sometime in 2019.

In the meantime, just because the regulators may not legally require a certain level of care and service for investors yet does not mean that you cannot demand such a level of service in order for a stockbroker or financial adviser to manage your investment account. It's your money. If they want to manage your assets, then they must meet your demands. Hopefully, by the end of this book, you will know more than them anyway and realize that you can easily manage you own money.

Classes of Costs and Fees
Commissions – Commissions are essentially sales charges you pay stockbrokers and/or insurance salesmen to purchase types of investment products, e.g., stock, bonds variable annuities, fixed indexed/equity indexed annuities.

Loads – Loads are essentially commissions charged by some mutual funds to purchase their mutual funds. Mutual fund companies often offer various classes of mutual funds shares with various levels of loads and shareholder rights.

Two of the most common classes of retail shares are "A" shares and "B" shares. "A" shares usually impose a "front-end" load, or sales charge at the time of purchase. The current maximum front-end load is 5.75 percent of the purchase. "B" shares usually often may impose a "back-end" load, or sales charge, if and when the "B" shares are redeemed from the mutual fund company.

Back-end loads may take various forms. Some mutual fund companies charge a flat rate over a specified period, e.g., 7 percent a year for 7 years. Other funds may charge back-end loads based on a sliding scale over a certain period of time, e.g., for 7 years, starting at 7 percent and diminishing 1 percent each year thereafter. Other popular back-load variations include vanishing back-loads due to a passage of time or vanishing back-loads due to the right to convert "B" shares to "A" shares after a period of time.

With the increasing popularity of 401(k) plans, 403(b) plans and other types of pension plans, mutual funds have begun offering retirement shares of their mutual funds. These retirement classes of shares, often designated as "R" or "K" shares, often charge lower annual fees and other costs.

12b-1 fees – These fees were originally approved to help cover the mutual funds' distribution and marketing costs. Given the fact that most mutual funds are now mega-million dollar entities that do not need such subsidies from customers, the only purpose 12b-1 fees serve today is to provide stockbrokers with annual payments to convince the stockbrokers not to move their customers and clients out of the fund company's funds. Just avoid such unfair fees by avoiding funds that charge 12b-1 fees. **Note**: Many retirement shares do not charge 12b-1 fees. Avoid those that do. There is just no reason to pay such 12b-1 fees.

InvestSense IQ: Each 1 percent in fees and other costs reduces an investor's end-return by approximately 17 percent over a twenty year period. With regard to fees, YOU get what you DON'T pay for.

Chapter Five
How Do I Evaluate a Mutual Fund's Returns?

Investors are constantly being bombarded with advertisements for various investment products, especially mutual funds. Most investment advertisements contain various return numbers and usually a couple of Morningstar's "stars" in large print, accompanied with a <u>lot</u> of small print and disclosures toward the end of the advertisement. If the advertisement is on television, ever notice how they always seem to speed up the small print at the end of the mutual fund and insurance advertisements?

Most investors are not aware that there are actually three types of returns that investors should know about-nominal, or stated returns; load-adjusted returns; and risk-adjusted returns. Nominal returns are always the annual return numbers that are in large print. Those are the numbers that mutual fund companies and stockbroker want you to focus on.

For example, let's assume that an investor purchased a share of a mutual fund at the beginning of the year. The share was worth $10 a share at the start of the year and worth $15 a share at the end of the year. The mutual fund company would probably run an ad claiming that the fund had a return of 50 percent for the year. But is that a fair and accurate representation of the return the investor "effectively" received?

There are four main types of mutual funds:

1. <u>Actively managed mutual funds</u>-these are mutual funds that are actively managed by teams of managers who pick and choose stocks and other investments to buy and sell for their shareholders. Advocates of active managed mutual funds claim that active management provides for better returns and better risk management. However, studies consistently prove that those claims are not supported by the evidence of historical performance. In fact, the most notable characteristic of these funds are their cost-inefficiency as a result of their excessive fees/costs and consistent underperformance relative to comparable passive/ index funds.

2. <u>Index mutual funds</u>-these are passively managed mutual funds which simply track a chosen stock market index, such as the S&P 500 or the Dow Jones Industrial Average, or some other investment index. The most notable characteristics of these funds are their cost-efficiency as a result of their consistently low fees/costs and consistently superior performance relative to that of comparable actively managed mutual funds.

3. <u>Exchange-traded mutual funds (ETFs)</u>-these are funds that can share characteristics of both actively managed funds and index funds. While actively managed funds and index funds are usually purchased directly from a fund company, ETFs are purchased on a stock market exchange. As a result, the investor usually pays a small commission on the purchase transaction.

ETFs started out as passive only investments. However, a number of actively managed ETFs have begun to appear, as ETFs have begun to grow increasingly popular among investors.

If ETFS share most of the same characteristics as regular mutual funds, why are they so popular, why are regular mutual funds not enough alone? ETFs are generally cost-efficient and tax-efficient. They also provide greater flexibility and more variety than most regular mutual funds. One final advantage of ETFs is that they can be traded during the day, which may help in managing market risk. Regular mutual funds can only be traded once a day, usually right after the markets close. Consequently, regular mutual funds can expose an investor to potentially greater risks than ETFs.

4. <u>Closed-end funds</u>-I'm not going to spend a lot of time on this type of mutual fund since most investors will never deal with these funds. Two things to know about closed-end funds:

(a) Like stocks, they are traded on stock market exchanges; and
(b) They are traded at a premium or a discount to their "inherent" value.

This is one of the primary reasons for some investors' interest in these type mutual funds.

Load-adjusted returns

1. <u>Front-end loads</u>-Actively managed mutual funds often charge a "front-end load", or sales charge, just to purchase their shares. The front-end load is usually based upon a percentage of the investor's original total purchase price. The front-end load is immediately deducted from the investor's total purchase price at the time the purchase is finalized.

The current legally allowed maximum front-end load charge is 5.75 percent. So, if an investor were to purchase $50,000 of an actively managed mutual fund that charged a front-end load of 5.75 percent, the mutual fund would immediately deduct $2,875 from the investor's money and invest the remaining $47,125 in the company's mutual fund.

The problem that many investors do not consider is the fact that a fund's front-end load means that they will start out behind the investor who is not forced to pay a front-end load. Assuming comparable returns over the life of the two investments, the investor who paid the front-end load will always trail the investor who did not pay a front-end load.

How much impact can a front-end load have on returns? Using our example, and assuming the two investments earn an annual return of 10 percent, the impact over a 10 and 20 year period would be as follows:

	5 Years	10 Years
No Load	$73,205	$117,897
5.75 Load%	$68,995	$111,118

So, in our example, after five years the load investor would be $4,210 behind the no-load investor, $6,779 behind the no-load investor after ten years. Larger initial investments would result in larger differences between the investors. Given all the available no-load options and their overall superior performance record, why would anyone choose to pay a front-end load for a mutual fund? More on that later.

Some mutual funds that impose a front-end load on purchases of their mutual funds offer "breakpoints, or reduced loads, based on the amount of an investor's purchase or cumulative purchases. Again, why pay any load fees for cost-inefficient mutual funds with excessive fees and poor performance records relative to no-load fees? Load-adjusted returns are provided online at several web sites, including Fidelity Research and Marketwatch.

2. <u>Back-end loads</u>-also known as "contingent deferred sales charges" (CDSC), these are sales charges that "might" be imposed if an investor attempts to redeem their shares before the expiration of a specified time period. When an investor purchases class "A" mutual fund shares that impose a front-end load, the mutual fund company uses the load to pay the stockbroker their commission.

When an investor purchases "B" shares, the mutual fund company does not charge an investor a load at the time of the initial purchase. The mutual fund company still has to pay the stockbroker his/her commission though. The contingent "back-end load" serves to ensure that the mutual fund company recovers any portion of the commissions they have yet to recover through a fund's fees.

"B" shares have another feature that investors need to know about and understand-conversion privileges. Some mutual fund companies allow "B" share owners to convert their shares to "A" shares after a certain period of time. In essence, once the mutual fund company has recouped the commission it paid to the stockbroker when an investor initially purchased their fund, the fund company then will allow the investor to convert their shares to "A" shares, which usually charge lower annual fees than "B" shares.

InvestSense IQ: Each 1 percent in fees and other costs reduces an investor's end-return by approximately 17 percent over a twenty year period. With regard to fees, YOU get what you DON'T pay for.

Risk-adjusted returns
A well-known saying is that investment return received is a function of investment risk assumed. The investment industry hates to hear any discussion about investment risk, especially when it involves

adjusting an investment's return to factor for the investment's risk. The standard response from the investment industry-"investor's cannot eat risk-adjusted returns."

I have always found the industry's response interesting. First, factoring in the management of investment risk often benefits actively managed funds by increasing their adjusted returns. Active management often produces a slightly higher return for investors, although usually not enough to overcome passive management's lower costs and consistent record of outperformance.

Second, actively managed mutual funds are definitely not shy about referencing their Morningstar "stars" score in their advertisements. When I point this out to stockbrokers and explain how Morningstar calculates their "stars, they usually quickly wander off. That's right; Morningstar relies heavily on a fund's risk-adjusted return in calculating and assigning a fund its "stars."

Morningstar does provide a fund's risk-adjusted return, you just to know where to look. A fund's risk and tax-adjusted performance are included in the fund's after-tax analysis on the Morningstar web site (morningstar.com).

Chapter Six
Asset Allocation and Market Timing

Risk management is one key aspects of successful investing. A key component of successful risk management is effective asset allocation, as it theoretically helps avoid significant losses. There are various asset allocation strategies that investors and wealth managers use. But first, let expose what asset allocation is not.

One of the "dirty little secrets" of the investment industry is their deliberate misrepresentation of the findings of a study on the importance of asset allocation. The study, commonly referred to as the BHB study after the three gentleman who conducted the study, found that asset allocation explained 93.6% of the *variation* in an investment portfolio's returns. The study made no representations about the determinants of an investment portfolio's returns, only the variations in a portfolio's returns.

The study examined three general types of investments - stocks, bonds and cash. Stocks are generally acknowledged as riskier than bonds, and bonds are generally acknowledged as being riskier than cash. So the BHB study should not come as a surprise to anyone. Higher allocations to stocks, as compared to bonds and cash, can be expected to increase a portfolio's overall volatility, or variation in returns.

Subsequent studies have documented the extent to which the BHB study's conclusions have been deliberately misrepresented. "Just get your investment portfolio's asset allocation right and the portfolio's performance will take care of itself." However, subsequent studies not only stressed the difference between performance returns and performance volatility, but also on the fact that

- about 75 percent of a typical fund's variation in returns comes from movements within the general market, with the balance split equally between the specific asset allocation and active, and

- a dynamic and strategic asset allocation is more effective than a "set-it-and-forget-it" static asset allocation program.

Investors who understand the true findings of the BHB study, and the fact that the study made no representations as to the determinants of a portfolio's actual returns, can better protect their financial security by detecting misrepresentations regarding the value of investment recommendations.

Allocation vs. Diversification

As mentioned earlier, one of the "secrets" of successful investing is to avoid significant losses. Asset allocation is one of the keys to avoiding significant losses, but only asset allocation that "effectively" diversifies an investor's portfolio.

One of the most common mistakes investors make is not understanding the difference between asset allocation and effective diversification. A portfolio may be allocated among various types/categories of investment, but still not be "effectively" diversified. "Effective" diversification is the aspect of a portfolio that prevents significant losses.

So how do you differentiate between asset allocation and diversification? Harry Markowitz won the Nobel Prize for his work in creating Modern Portfolio Theory (MPT). MPT introduced the concept that the overall risk of an investment portfolio could be reduced by effectively diversifying an investment portfolio. Markowitz argued that the cornerstone of effective diversification was the combination of assets with varying levels of correlation of investment returns.

"To reduce risk it is necessary to avoid a portfolio whose securities are all highly correlated with each other . One hundred securities whose returns rise and fall in near unison afford little more than the uncertain return of a single security. Effective diversification depends not only on the number of assets in a trust portfolio, but also on the ways and degrees in which their responses to economic events tend to reinforce, cancel or neutralize one another."[13]

So, a 401(k) portfolio consisting of a couple of large cap funds, a couple of small cap funds, a fixed income fund and one or two international funds does not guarantee that the portfolio is "effectively " diversified. In fact, it is more likely that the portfolio is <u>not</u> effectively diversified, as equity-based mutual funds, both domestic and international equity funds, have shown a definite trend of increasing correlations of returns over the past decade or so.

Given the importance of correlation of returns between investments, how do investors find out what the correlations of returns are between the investments in their portfolios? Unfortunately, due to the various combinations of investments and the resulting number of possible correlation numbers, investors basically have to perform the correlation calculations themselves. There are several sites online that help calculate correlation calculations, but many of these calculation programs are restricted to investment professionals.

For investors just trying to perform calculations for themselves, I often suggest that they can compare the R-squared numbers that Morningstar provides for mutual funds in comparison to the Standard & Poor's 500 Index (S&P 500). While the S&P 500 may not otherwise be an appropriate benchmark for the two funds in question, the funds' S&P 500 R-squared numbers can then be compared to provide a rough estimate of the correlation between the two fund's returns for the period chosen.

Investors can also perform actual correlation calculations by using the CORREL function on Microsoft Excel. Investors can obtain monthly and/or annual return numbers by referring to the "Performance" tab on a mutual fund's page at morningstar.com. In order to gain more meaningful numbers and hopefully prevent skew, it is strongly recommended that five or ten years of a fund's returns be used for performing the calculations.

The Great Market Timing Debate

Once you have your investment portfolio allocated and effectively diversified, the question is whether to ever modify the allocations in terms of the type or percentage of an investment. One of the most debated topics in the world of investing is "market timing." I think one of the reasons for the debate about market timing has to do with the lack of a clear definition and understanding of what market timing involves. The classic definition of "market timing" is allocating your investments such that at any point in time, an investor is either 100 percent in the stock market or 100 percent out of the market. 100 percent in or 100 percent out, with no in-between.

The basic concept is being able to perfectly time the movements in the stock markets, to maximize profits. The classic definition of market timing is generally dismissed as futile and costly by most experts. Advocates of that school of thought generally dismiss any asset allocation concept that involves any reallocation of an investor's assets once an initial asset allocation has been made as "market timing." This is commonly referred to as the "buy-and-hold" approach to investing by its proponents, or "buy-forget-and regret" by its opponents.

Opponents of "buy-and-hold" investing point to the historical evidence that shows that the stock markets are cyclical, alternating between strong, or "bull," markets and weaker, or "bear," markets. Small market drops of approximately ten percent or so are often referred to as "corrections, "with the "bear" designation reserved for larger market drops of twenty percent or more.

As mentioned earlier, investment icon Charles Ellis has stated that successful investing is actually a *defensive* process, with the key to successful investing being the avoidance of significant investment losses.[14] With that in mind, many, myself included, view so-called strategic asset allocation as a proactive, defensive, wealth preservation tool rather than "market timing."

There are various ways that people implement such a defensive wealth preservation program. Some do not actually do any reallocation of actual assets, but rather use so-called "protective puts" to protect against significant drops in value of whatever portion of their assets they decide to protect. If an investor does suffer a loss in the value of their portfolio, the protective puts serve as insurance and replace such lost value.

Another popular strategic, defensive asset allocation program is one that was suggested by investment legend Benjamin Graham, often called the "Father of Modern Investing." Graham's suggestion was simple to implement and understand:

1. Divide an investment portfolio 50/50 between stocks and bonds.
2. Adjust the allocations based on the investor's feelings about the strength of the stock market and overall economic conditions.
3. Continue making adjustments in the allocations as appropriate, but never let the percentage allocated to either stocks or bonds get higher than 75 percent or lower than 25 percent.

One of the attractive aspects of Graham's system was that he was not trying to perfectly time the stock market, just ensuring that an investor would always be in the stock market, but at a level they were comfortable with in hopes of avoiding significant losses.

This is a subject that every investor has to decide for themselves. Some choose "buy-and-hold" or "set, forget, and regret." Others choose a more proactive, defensive, yet reasonable approach to minimize investment losses. For what it is worth, the Graham system allowed many investors to avoid the catastrophic 40 percent-plus losses sustained in the 2008 bear market, while at the same time having exposure in the market to more fully benefit from the market's eventual recovery.

In making that decision, I will present one more piece of evidence that investors should consider. The investment industry likes to argue that investors suffer significant losses by making changes in their portfolio allocations.

As an attorney, I known that there are always two sides to a story, and more often than not, the differences are very significant. Therefore, in the interests of fairness, I will inform you that **various studies have documented the fact that avoiding losses has a much greater impact than missing potential returns.**

According to one recent study, missing the "best" 10, 20 and 100 days on the market, defined as the Dow Jones Industrial Average ("DJIA"), during the period 1990-2006 would have reduced an investor's terminal wealth by approximately 38 percent, 56.8 percent and 93.8 percent, respectively. Conversely, avoiding the worst 10, 20 and 100 days on the DJIA over the same period would have improved an investor's terminal wealth by 70.1 percent, 140.6 percent and 1,619.1 percent, respectively.[15]

Brokers will usually counter that those figures ignore the potential tax consequences. With regard to a taxable account that would be true. But that would not be true in a tax-deferred account such as a 401(k), 4013(b) or IRA account, where reallocations in such accounts are generally not taxable until withdrawals are actually made. Think that investors who lost 40 percent or more in their retirement accounts during the 2000-2002 and 2007-2008 bear markets wish they had utilized some proactive, defensive strategies to reduce their losses? Think they wish someone had educated them on the existence of such sound and proven strategies?

Again, no one can perfectly time the markets to achieve optimal returns. However, that should not be an investor's goal.

Smart investors would be wise to heed the advice of Benjamin Graham, who warned that "the essence of investment management is the management of risks, not the management of returns." Or, as noted by industry expert Charles Ellis, "the ultimate outcome of wealth management is determined by who can lose the fewest points, not by who can win the most." Why? Simply because money lost in market downturns cannot fully participate in the eventual market recovery.

Chapter Seven
Putting It All Together:
The Active Management Value Ratio™3.0

So we have various factors that investors need to use to analyze available investment products and strategies. How do we put them together into an effective investment portfolio and wealth management strategy to help better protect one's financial security?

First, we take our various return calculations. With retail fund shares, funds that impose a front-end load will have all three return calculations: nominal, load-adjusted and risk-adjusted. No-load funds will only have two return calculations-nominal returns and risk-adjusted.

The Active Management Value Ratio™ 3.0 (AMVR) metric allows investors, fiduciaries, pension plan sponsors and attorneys to calculate the cost-efficiency of actively managed mutual funds. As a securities/ERISA attorney, I have always found it incredible that ERISA (Employees Retirement Income Security Act), America's primary retirement security act, allowed employers to shift the risk of saving and managing for one's retirement onto usually inexperienced employees, and yet did not require such employers to provide the workers and pension plan participants with a meaningful formal investment education program.

As a result, there is a general consensus within America that most employees are not "retirement ready" and, as a result, far too Americans face a bleak retirement. That is one of the primary reasons I decided to write this book. As a securities/ERISA attorney, a former securities/RIA compliance director, a CERTIFIED FINANCIAL PLANNER™ professional, and an Accredited Wealth Management Advisor[SM], I knew I had the knowledge and experience to provide investors, fiduciaries, pension plan sponsors and plan participants with information to improve their accumulation and preservation of investment and retirement assets instead of the glorified and biased marketing spiel with which far too many investors and pensions plans and plan participants are provided.

The Elements of AMVR

As an attorney, I put a lot of emphasis on evidence. The AMVR is based on academic research by industry icons and long-standing legal standards.

When I work with securities/ERISA attorneys, I explain my four-point investment fiduciary liability system:

1. The Supreme Court has stated that the Restatement (Third) of Trusts (Restatement) is a valuable resource in resolving fiduciary issues, especially involving ERISA questions.[16]
2. Section 90 of ERISA (aka the Prudent Investor Rule), comment b, states that fiduciaries have a duty to be cost-conscious.[17]
3. Section 90 of ERISA, comment f, states that in selecting investments for pension plans and other accounts, fiduciaries have a duty to choose investment that provide the highest level of return for a given level of costs and risks or, conversely, the lowest level of costs and risks for a given level of return.[18]
4. Section 90 of ERISA, comment h(2). states that fiduciaries should not choose or recommend actively managed mutual funds unless it is "realistic" to assume that such funds will produce sufficient returns to cover the extra costs and risk commonly associated with such funds, i.e., such funds are cost-efficient.[19]

And there is the rub, the investment industry's "dirty little secret." Investment advertisements and mutual fund companies love to tout investment return numbers. However, even the numbers they tout are often highly suspect and misleading...and they know it! Advertisements touting "we're #1" or "we're the best" are common, based on nominal return numbers. How many investment advertisements have you ever seen touting a fund's cost-efficiency? fund?" The overwhelming majority of actively-managed funds are simply not cost-efficient.

My focus on cost-efficiency is based on the research of investment icons such as Charles D. Ellis and Burton G. Malkiel:

- *The incremental fees for an actively managed mutual fund relative to its incremental returns should always be compared to the fees of a comparable index fund relative to its returns. When you do this, you'll quickly see that the incremental fees for active management are really, really high-on average, over 100% of incremental returns.*[20]
- *Increasing numbers of clients will realize that in toe-to-toe competition versus near-equal competitors, most active managers will not and cannot recover the costs and fees they charge."*[21]
- *Past performance is not helpful in predicting future returns. The two variables that do the best job in predicting future performance of [mutual funds] are expense ratios and turnover.*[22]
- *There is strong evidence that the vast majority of active managers are unable to produce excess returns that cover their costs.*[23]

With that information in mind, I created a simple metric, the Active Management Value Ratio™ 3.0 (AMVR). The AMVR allows investors, investment fiduciaries and attorneys to determine whether an actively managed mutual fund is cost-efficient, and therefore compliant with the standards set out in the Restatement's Prudent Investor Rule. It is usually about this time that stockbrokers point out that they are not required to adhere to fiduciary standards, not required to put a customer's financial interest ahead of their own.

That's not exactly true though. Depending on the circumstances, courts can, and have, imposed a fiduciary on stockbrokers and other financial advisers to prevent manifest injustice against an investor. For example, where courts have determined that the stockbroker has essentially assumed control over a customer's account and/or an investor lacked the knowledge and/or experience to understand and independently evaluate the advice and recommendations given to them by their stockbroker or financial adviser.

Calculating the AMVR™ 3.0

Active Management Value Ratio™ 3.0

	Fees	Total Fees	Active Expense Ratio	Annual Return	Returns
Active Fund					
Expense Ratio		0.64	5.40	15.47%	Nominal
Trading Costs	25%	0.30	0.30	14.11%	Load-Adj
Total Costs		0.94	5.70	12.94%	Risk-Adj
Benchmark Fund					
Expense Ratio		0.17	0.17	15.34%	Nominal
Trading Costs	3%	0.04	0.04	14.06%	Risk-Adj
Total Costs		0.21	0.21		
IC/IR		0.73	5.49	-1.12	
% Fees/% Return		77%	96%	NA	

Incremental Return Analysis

The actively-managed fund actually outperforms the Vanguard fund based on nominal, or stated, return. However, the actively-managed fund imposes a front-end load/fee of 5.75 percent on purchases of retail shares, which is immediately deducted from an investor's account.

As a result, if both produce the same nominal return over time, the load fund investor will never receive the stated nominal fee since their account has less money to benefit from the fund's future returns. In this case, an investor would have received a five-year annualized return of only 14.11 percent over the period from October 1, 2013 to September 29, 2018, not the stated nominal return of 15.47 percent over that same period. Note: All return numbers stated herein cover the same period.) You get what you DON'T pay for!

A common saying in the investment world is that returns are a function of risk. Therefore, in order to get a more accurate evaluation of a fund, the fund's returns need to be adjusted for the level of risk the fund assumed in achieving the indicated returns. In my practice, I use Morningstar's risk-adjusted return methodology.

However, here the actively-managed fund underperforms the Vanguard fund on both a load-adjusted and risk-adjusted basis. As a result, this actively managed fund is imprudent based on returns alone when compared to the Vanguard benchmark fund.

Incremental Cost Analysis
When an actively-managed fund fails to provide a positive incremental return, there is obviously no reason to perform an incremental cost analysis. Investors invest to make money, not lose money. However, I want to do an incremental cost analysis for the sake of example.

Simple, straightforward basic math. "My, Dear, Aunt, Sally" from our elementary school math days. All of the information needed to perform an AMVR analysis is available for free online at sites such as morningstar.com, marketwatch.com, and yahoo.com. I like to add trading costs into the AMVR analysis based on Malkiel's findings.

In this example, the nominal incremental cost between the two funds is 73 basis points (0.73). (Note: A basis point is 1/100th (.01) of one percent.) That means that the actively-managed fund's incremental, or excess, costs constitutes 77 percent of the fund's total costs, with the investor receiving absolutely no positive return for such costs. Investors need to remember that each additional 1 percent in fees and costs reduces an investor's end-return by approximately 17 percent over 20 years. That loss would also need to be adjusted on a percentage basis based on the investment's overall percentage allocation within the investor's total portfolio.

Closet Indexing
Closet indexing is a serious problem in investment industries around the world. Closet indexing refers to situations where an actively-managed fund claims that it offers actively-managed funds and

charges significantly higher fees based on the purported benefits of active management. However, more often than not, such funds simply track the performance of a comparable, less expensive index fund, wasting an investor's money. Again, you get what you DON"T pay for.

To evaluate the impact of possible closet indexing, I perform a second incremental cost analysis using Ross Miller's Active Expense Ratio (AER).[24] It is not necessary to perform an AER analysis to benefit from an AMVR analysis. I simply perform the extra analysis due to my clientele and to further guarantee the cost-efficiency of an actively managed mutual fund.

A simple explanation of the AER is that the metric uses a fund's R-squared number, or correlation of return number, to determine the extent to which an actively-managed fund tracks a comparable market index or index fund. The metric then adjusts a fund's incremental cost number to reflect the effective cost of the fund in light of the extent to which the fund's performance is properly attributable to the active management of the fund, rather than a market index or comparable index fund.

In the immediate case, the fund's high R-squared number, 96, combined with the level of the fund's incremental costs, results in an effective annual expense ratio of 5.40 percent, significantly higher than the Vanguard fund's annual expense ratio of 0.17. The resulting incremental cost constitutes approximately 96 percent of the actively-managed fund's AER-adjusted effective annual expense ratio. Once again, high incremental fees combined with absolutely no positive incremental return results in a fund that is not cost-efficient.

Chapter Eight
Avoiding Investment "Games"

When people ask me what kind of law I practice, I tell them that I am a wealth preservation attorney. To me, wealth preservation consists of three separate areas of wealth management - accumulation, protection and preservation. Wealth preservation involves several areas of the law, including risk management, both in terms of investment portfolios and general liability; estate planning; asset protection; retirement distribution planning; and other related areas of wealth management. The primary focus is to address each of these areas, analyze a client's current situation, and reduce or eliminate any unnecessary exposure to actual or potential losses.

With regard to wealth management, I analyze a clients' current investment portfolio in terms of overall suitability and efficiency, in terms of both cost and risk management. I draw heavily on over twenty years of experience in the area of quality of financial advice.

I primarily use four metrics, three of which are proprietary – the Active Management Value Ratio, Miller's Active Expense Ratio, the Fiduciary IQ, and a stress test. Relying on these metrics, we often find situations where clients are paying fees that are often 300-400 higher than necessary to get similar, or better, performance from less expensive investment options.

The key to effective wealth preservation is not to view wealth preservation in isolation, but rather as part of a comprehensive wealth management plan. The key is also to create a strong team of professionals experienced in these areas and work towards a client's goals and needs.

Investment Industry "Games"
In my experience as a securities compliance director and a securities and wealth preservation attorney, I have seen a lot of "games" often used by the financial services industry. In most cases, the "games" are employed to provide more compensation to the financial adviser at the investor's expense.

Five of the most common "games," or deceptive practices, used in the industry are:

1. <u>Inverse pricing by variable annuities</u> - This refers to the practice by the variable annuity industry to base their annual fees on the total value of the variable annuity rather than the cost of their legal obligation to the annuity owner, a practice commonly referred to as inverse pricing since the fee is not based on the actual potential cost to the variable annuity issuer. Most variable annuities obligate the variable annuity issuer to pay the annuity owner's heirs the greater of the value of the variable annuity or the owner's actual contributions.

Given the historical trends of the stock market, it is unlikely that the value of the variable annuity will be less than the owner's contributions. Consequently, inverse pricing essentially guarantees the variable annuity issuer a substantial windfall at the owner's expense. Most variable issuers charge an annual fee of 2 percent or more, despite the fact the fact that one well-known study estimated that the actual value of the protection for which the fee is charged is approximately 0.10 percent.

The annual fee charges are even more egregious when one considers that each 1 percent of additional 1 percent of investment fees reduces an investor's return by approximately 17 percent over a twenty year. When you add the additional fees for a variable annuity's sub-accounts, the total fees on variable annuities often exceed 3 percent or more, effectively reducing an investor's end return by over 50 percent or more. A recent addition to the annuity product line is the so-called fixed-income indexed, or equity-based index annuity. While these products have a number of negative issues, the leading issue is the fact that such products come with various features that seriously limit the real return that investors can achieve. For more information on these issues, please read the white paper, "Variable Annuities" on the "CommonSense InvestSense" blog, (investsense.com).

Wealth preservation "best practice": Variable annuities and fixed indexed annuities-just say no!

2. <u>"Pseudo" or false diversification</u> - This issue refers to the practice

of providing investors with investment recommendations among various types of investments, e.g., large cap growth funds, small cap value funds, international funds and leading an investor to believe that the recommendations will provide the investor with a diversified investment portfolio and protection against downside risk. But looks can be misleading.

Effective diversification provides investors with both upside potential and downside protection against substantial losses. However, given the high correlation of returns among most equity-based investments, both domestic and international equity investments, the recommendations often do not provide the protection supposedly provided by diversification at all.

Looking at the five-year (2009-2014) correlation data for five equity-based categories often used in asset allocation recommendations, (large cap growth, large cap value, small cap growth, small cap value, and a popular international index, MSCI's EAFE), the pattern of high correlation is obvious:

94 percent correlation between LCG-LCV
91 percent correlation between LCG-SCG
90 percent correlation between LCG-SCV
87 percent correlation between LCG-EAFE
90 percent correlation between LCV-SCG
94 percent correlation between LCV-SCV
86 percent correlation between LCV-EAFE
97 percent correlation between SCG-SCV
75 percent correlation between SCG-EAFE
76 percent correlation between SCV-EAFE

Looking at the ten-year (2005-2014) correlation data for the same categories further demonstrated the high correlation pattern for equity-based investments:

92 percent correlation between LCG-LCV
92 percent correlation between LCG-SCG
87 percent correlation between LCG-SCV
87 percent correlation between LCG-EAFE

88 percent correlation between LCV-SCG
93 percent correlation between LCV-SCV
87 percent correlation between LCV-EAFE
95 percent correlation between SCG-SCV
79 percent correlation between SCG-EAFE
77 percent correlation between SCV-EAFE

Bottom line, in most case "pseudo," or false diversification simply provides an investor with nothing more than a false sense of security and an unnecessarily expensive index fund, with reduced returns due to the excessive fees.

Wealth preservation "best practice": Investors should always ask their financial adviser to prepare a correlation of return analysis for both their existing investment portfolio and the investment portfolio being recommended. After all, without a correlation of returns analysis, how can a financial adviser know whether his/her recommendations are in the best interests of the investor?

3. <u>Closet index funds</u> - "Closet index", or "index hugger" funds are mutual funds with high R-squared ratings. Their high R-squared rating indicates that investors may be able to achieve similar or better returns at a significantly lower cost by using index-based investments.

Morningstar defines R-squared as a measure of the correlation of the portfolio's returns to the benchmark's returns. An R-squared of 100 indicates that all movements of a portfolio can be explained by movements in the benchmark. Conversely, a low R-squared indicates that very few of the portfolio's movements can be explained by movements in its benchmark index. Effective diversification involves combining investments with low correlations of return so that the investments provide downside protection against large losses, regardless of economic or market conditions.

There is no universally accepted R-squared rating level for classification of a fund as a closet index fund. Some use a rating of 95 as the threshold rating, while some use a score as low as 80-85.

InvestSense classifies any mutual fund with an R-squared rating of 90 or above as a "closet index" fund. This position is based upon our belief that the ability to achieve the same or similar returns of a benchmark index fund without the higher fees generally associated with actively managed mutual funds, often 3-4 times higher than a comparable index fund, is more conducive to effective wealth management and preservation.

Wealth preservation "best practice": Do not invest in "closet index" funds, funds with R-squared ratings of 90 or higher.

4. <u>Cost-inefficient actively managed mutual funds</u> - One of my specialties is fiduciary law. One of the primary duties of a fiduciary is to manage any money entrusted to them in a prudent manner, always putting the best interests of the client first. One of the primary aspects of prudence is to avoid unnecessary fees and expenses.

There are two ways of evaluating the fees charged by actively managed mutual funds. The first involves calculating the effective cost of such fees based up on the actual active management component of a fund. The higher a fund's R-squared number is, the lower the contribution of the active management component of such fund.

Since closet index funds have a small active management component, their effective fees will be significantly higher than their stated annual fees. A study by Professor Ross Miller found that the effective cost of active management generally exceeded a fund's stated annual expense, often by as much as 300-400 percent.

A second way of evaluating the fees of actively managed mutual funds is to use our proprietary metric, the Active Management Value Ratio 3.0™ (AMVR) to evaluate the cost efficiency of a mutual fund. The AMVR is a powerful, yet simple, cost/benefit analysis that requires nothing more than the ability to perform simple subtraction and division. And yet, the AMVR often indicates that actively managed mutual funds are cost inefficient, as the incremental, or extra, return provided by actively managed mutual funds, if any, is exceeded by the fund's incremental, or extra, costs.

Wealth preservation "best practice": Avoid "closet index" mutual funds and take the time to calculate the AMVR 3.0 rating for mutual funds currently owned and/or being considered as potential investments.

5. <u>Relative returns</u> - aka the "we're number 1" scam. Investment ads and advisers like to tout that their product has had the best performance compared to their competitors. This comparative, or "relative," performance allows an investment company or financial adviser to make such a claim, even though the actual return was lackluster or even negative.

This is a common practice after a down year for the stock market, such as the bear markets of 2000-2002 and 2008, when many mutual funds suffered losses of 30 percent or more. The fact that one's mutual fund suffered a 30 percent return while another fund suffered a 32 percent is hardly cause for celebration.

Investors need to focus on funds that have provided consistent absolute returns. Absolute returns are simply the actual returns that an investment has provided over time. An investment with a consistent history of positive absolute returns means that an investor has not only benefited from the returns themselves, but also from the compounding of such returns over time.

Wealth preservation "best practice": Remember that mutual fund advertisements are touting their relative returns which generally do not represent the returns that investors are actually going to receive Investors are better served by focusing on a fund's ability to provide consistent and positive annual absolute returns.

Chapter Nine
Annuities

As you will read shortly, I believe annuities, particularly variable annuities and fixed indexed/equity indexed annuities, are among the most abused investment/insurance products offered in the investment industry. Both products are annually among the top five investment products among consumer complaints. For those reasons, I consider both variable annuities and fixed indexed annuities among the leading wealth preservation "saboteurs" in the investment industry.

One of the first posts I published on my consumer investor protection blog, "CommonSense InvestSense," (investsense.com), was the following post. It has been, and still is, consistently the most viewed post on the blog, often with over a hundred hits a month. Based on what readers have told me, they like the format of the post, written in a way that provides the common sales spiel used in selling these products, both in terms of what is said and what is not disclosed.

Many people, stockbrokers included, do not truly understand these products. But stockbrokers and broker-dealers definitely know that both pay large commissions, in some case 6-7 percent compared to the usual 4-5 percent for actively managed mutual funds.

There is a common expression in the investment and insurance industries-"annuities are sold, not bought." This post will explain why there is a lot of truth in that saying.

"Variable Annuities
Reading Between the Marketing Lines

"Variable annuities are one of the most overhyped, most oversold, and least understood investment products."

"Annuities are sold, not bought.

Variable annuity salesmen use various sales pitches to convince investors to purchase a variable annuity. However, as is often the case, what is unsaid is often as important, if not more important, than what is said. This information gap can have serious financial consequences. For purposes of this article, all references to variable annuities shall only refer to non-qualified variable annuities, those annuities that do not qualify for special treatment under the Internal Revenue Code.

Basic Structure of Annuities
Before analyzing some of the popular sales pitches used by variable annuity salesmen, it is important to understand the basic structure of a variable annuity. A variable annuity can be described as an insurance contract wrapped around mutual fund subaccounts. The presence of the insurance "wrapper" allows the variable annuity to provide tax-deferred growth.

Variable annuities typically charge two primary fees, an annual insurance fee and an annual subaccount management fee. The insurance fee usually consists of a mortality and expense (M & E) charge, usually in the range of 1.25-1.40 percent of the accumulated value of the variable annuity, and an administrative fee, usually in the range of 0.15-0.20 percent of the accumulated value of the variable annuity.

The M & E charge covers the guaranteed death benefit (GDB), which ensures that in the event that the owner of the variable annuity dies before annuitizing the variable annuity, his/her heirs will receive no less than the amount that the owner had invested in the variable annuity. The M & E charge also covers commission payments and general overhead expenses. The administrative fee covers various administrative expenses.

The subaccount management fee is charged for the professional management of the subaccount, much like the annual management fee charged by mutual funds. Subaccount management fees can vary depending on the type of account, with management fees typically falling within the 0.80-1.00 percent range.

The total annual fee charged on most variable annuities is approximately 2-3 percent of the overall value of the variable annuity. When compared to an average annual fee of 1 percent for actively managed mutual funds, 0.45 percent for passively managed mutual funds, and the typically low annual fees for exchange traded funds (ETFs), it is easy to see why the high fees and expenses associated with variable annuities are criticized, especially when their drag on long term performance is factored in.

Annuity Sales Pitches
So why do people continue to invest in variable annuities? Remember, annuities are sold, not bought. An analysis of some of the sales pitches used by variable annuity salesmen, in terms of what is said and what is unsaid, may prove helpful.

What's said: "Variable annuities offer tax deferred growth."

What's unsaid: There are a number of investment accounts (e.g., 401(k) accounts, IRA accounts, Keogh accounts, SIMPLE accounts) that offer tax deferred growth without the high fees and expenses associated with variable annuities. Even investors in stocks, mutual funds, and ETFs can achieve virtual tax-deferred growth as long as they do not actively trade their accounts and they choose investments with low turnover rates (e.g., passively managed funds such as index funds and most ETFs) and low income pay-outs.

The value of the tax-deferred growth offered by variable annuities is reduced by the effect of the high fees and expenses associated with variable annuities. Various studies have been done comparing the cost of investing in variable annuities to the cost of investing in mutual funds. These studies have generally concluded that in most cases it takes a minimum of 15-20 years, in some cases over forty years, for the owner of a variable annuity to break-even from the fees and expenses of variable annuities. In some cases, the owner of the variable annuity may never break-even.

An article by Dr. William Reichenstein of Baylor University provides an excellent in-depth analysis of the effects of fees on the overall return realized by variable annuity and mutual fund investors.

Among Dr. Reichenstein's findings were that the typical variable annuity, with a fee of 2 percent or more and an annual contract fee of $20-$30, is the least effective investment for investors.[26]

The value of the tax-deferred growth offered by variable annuities is also reduced by the tax aspects of a variable annuity as compared to a mutual fund. Tax-deferred does not mean tax-free. Sooner or later, the variable annuity owner or his/her beneficiaries will have to pay income tax on the capital appreciation within the variable annuity. Mutual fund owners can often use the capital gains tax rates to reduce the taxes on their mutual funds. Variable annuity owners cannot use the capital gains tax rate, as disbursements from variable annuities are taxed as ordinary income, which usually results in more tax liability and less money for the variable annuity owner or his/her beneficiaries

What's said: "You don't pay sales charges when you purchase a variable annuity, so all of your money goes to work for you, unlike mutual funds that charge front-end sales charges, and stocks and ETFs, which require an investor to pay costly brokerage commissions."

What's Unsaid: There are excellent no-load mutual funds that perform as well as, and often better than, variable annuity subaccounts. These no-load mutual funds usually charge annual management fees far less that those charged for variable annuity subaccounts, especially passively managed mutual funds such as index funds. Investors purchasing stocks and ETFs can use discount brokers to greatly reduce the amount of any brokerage commissions.

The statement that variable annuity owners pay no sales charges is misleading. Variable annuity salesmen do receive a commission, usually in the range of 6-7 percent of the total amount invested in the variable annuity. While a purchaser of a variable annuity is not directly assessed a front-end sales charge or a brokerage commission, the variable annuity owner does reimburse the insurance company for the commission that was paid. The primary source of such reimbursement is through the variable annuity's various fees and charges, particularly the M & E charge.

To ensure that the cost of commissions paid is recovered, the insurance company typically imposes surrender charges on a variable annuity owner who tries to cash out of the variable annuity before the expiration of a certain period of time. The terms of these surrender charges vary, but a typical surrender charge schedule might provide for an initial surrender charge of 7 percent for withdrawals during the first year, decreasing 1 percent each year thereafter until the eighth year, when the surrender charges would end. There are some surrender charge schedules that charge a flat rate, such as 7 percent, over the entire surrender charge period.

One recent variable annuity innovation that has caused regulators a great deal of concern has been the so-called "bonus" annuities. These products have been marketed in such a way that the public may believe that they receive a free bonus, usually in the range of 3-4 percent of their investment, upon their purchase of the annuity. In truth, the insurance company sponsoring the bonus annuity simply increases the term and/or the amount of the surrender charges to recover the "bonus." These bonus annuities continue to be the subject of much scrutiny due to their potential to mislead and deceive the public into thinking that they are receiving something that they really are not receiving.

Prospective annuity purchasers should always study the surrender charge schedule to minimize potential costs. Since surrender charge schedules often reflect the amount of commissions paid to the variable annuity salesman, an investor can compare the commission paid on a variable annuity (typically 6-7 percent) and the commission charged by front-end load mutual funds (typically 4-5 percent).

<u>What's said</u>: "Variable annuities offer a guaranteed death benefit (GDB) that ensures that the variable annuity owner's heirs will get no less than the amount of money that the variable annuity owner invested in the variable annuity.

<u>What's unsaid</u>: Most variable annuities discontinue the GDB once the variable annuity owner reaches a certain age. Furthermore, a variable annuity owner also generally loses the GDB if the owner elects to annuitize the variable annuity in order to receive the guaranteed

lifetime income benefits. The potential loss of the GDB is a factor tat should always be considered.

The value of the GDB itself is questionable. Variable annuities are intended to be long term investments. Given the long term historical performance of the stock market, it is highly unlikely that a variable annuity owner will need to use the GDB since, over the long term, the accumulated value of the variable annuity will probably exceed the amount of the GDB.

In his landmark study, annuity expert , Moshe Milevsky, found that the inherent benefit of the annual M&E fee for the GDB was between one and ten basis points, while the variable annuity companies routinely charge a M&E fee more that is ten times more, or higher.[28] Dr. Reichenstein's study produced similar findings.

Another interesting fact about the M & E charge is that while the GDB in most variable annuities only insures the variable annuity owner's investment in the variable annuity, the principal, the M & E charge is calculated based upon the accumulated value of the of the variable annuity, which includes both the principal and all capital appreciation within the annuity. This would seem to be clearly inequitable to the variable annuity owner who is forced to pay a higher amount of M & E charges as the value of the variable annuity increases, with no corresponding increase in the insurance company's obligation to the variable annuity owner.

For an additional fee, some insurance companies do offer a benefit that steps-up the amount of the GDB to the overall value of the variable annuity on certain anniversary dates. Given the unlikely need to use the GDB, the value of yet another layer of cost is equally questionable.

What's said: "Variable annuities can provide a lifetime stream of income, guaranteeing that you'll never run out of money to live on.

What's unsaid: To get the lifetime stream of income, the variable annuity owner generally has to annuitize the variable annuity. Upon annuitization, the variable annuity owner will receive a monthly payment, with the amount of the payment being based upon the owner's age and the settlement option that was chosen. The decision to annuitize should only be made after consideration of all of the consequences of such a decision.

Upon annuitization, the variable annuity owner gives up control of the annuity's assets. Even more important, depending on the settlement options offered by the insurance company and the settlement option chosen by the variable annuity owner, once the variable annuity is annuitized the insurance company, not the owner's heirs, will receive any money left in the annuity when the owner dies. Some variable annuities may require the owner of a variable annuity to annuitize their annuity upon reaching a certain age. Prospective variable annuity purchasers should always check the terms of a variable annuity being considered to see if the annuity contains such forced annuitization language, as it could frustrate an investor's estate plans.

Annuitization is, in essence, a gamble. The insurance company is hoping that the variable annuity owner dies before depleting all of the assets in the annuity, in which case the insurance company may receive the balance remaining in the annuity. The annuity owner, on the other hand, is gambling that they will live long enough to deplete the assets in their annuity.

What's said: "You can roll money over from your 401(k) or other retirement account into an IRA and then purchase a variable annuity for such account. You'll continue to receive tax deferred growth of your money and you'll get the safety of the guaranteed death benefit."

What's unsaid: Qualified plans, e.g., 401(k) plans, and IRAs already offer tax deferred growth. Consequently, purchasing a variable annuity within an IRA simply adds the high fees and expenses of the variable annuity without providing the investor with any meaningful additional benefits.

Many people work hard during their lifetime to accumulate funds not only for their retirement, but also to create an estate to leave to their heirs. Annuitization can result in an insurance company, not one's heirs, inheriting the results of one's hard work. While IRA owners must begin to take disbursements from an IRA once they reach a certain age, the balance remaining in the IRA at the owner's death passes to their designated beneficiaries. There are also various ways to minimize the amount of the required disbursements from an IRA so that the IRA assets can provide maximum benefits to one's children, grandchildren and beyond.

Placing a variable annuity within an IRA may result in a forced annuitization because of the required disbursements from an IRA at 70½ or because of language in the variable annuity requiring annuitization at a certain age or upon the occurrence of some event. Such a forced annuitization may result in consequences unintended, and undesired, by the IRA owner, including the owner's heirs' loss of their inheritance.

The questionable value of the GDB has already been discussed. The GDB is simply insurance. An investor who needs insurance and the GDB it provides should buy insurance, but through more cost effective options, such as term insurance.

What's said: "You'll have access to your money at all times since variable annuities typically allow an owner to withdraw up to 10% from their annuity annually, after the first year, without any penalty."

What's unsaid: The insurance company's decision to waive any penalties does not change the fact that all withdrawals from a variable annuity result in tax consequences. Withdrawals of gains from variable annuities are taxed as ordinary income. Variable annuity owners cannot use the capital gains tax rates to reduce their tax liability. In addition, withdrawals made by an owner prior to reaching the age of 59½ are generally subject to a penalty tax equal to 10% of the amount withdrawn.

Many variable annuities allow an owner to withdraw more than 10% in a limited number of circumstances. In the event that unanticipated circumstances arise during the period that the variable annuity's surrender charges are applicable, and such circumstances are not among those specified for allowing withdrawals beyond the insurance company's annual allowance, the variable annuity owner may have to pay the applicable surrender charges in addition to the ordinary income and penalty taxes.

What's said: "If you're ever dissatisfied with the performance of your variable annuity, you can switch to another variable annuity without paying any taxes."

What's unsaid: Tax-free exchanges, known as "1035 exchanges," present a number of issues. Both the NASD and the SEC have made questionable variable annuity sales tactics, including 1035 exchanges, a priority.

There are reports that 1035 exchanges account for a significant portion of annual variable annuity sales.[28] Brokers and advisors like 1035 exchanges since they result in new commissions for the broker or the advisor. Variable annuity owners contemplating such an exchange should note that any 1035 exchange made while the existing variable annuity is subject to surrender charges will result in the owner having to pay such surrender charges. In addition, if the new variable annuity imposes surrender charges, those surrender charges begin anew. Consequently, prior to making a 1035 exchange, a variable annuity owner whose annuity is free of surrender charges should carefully consider the costs and the limitations that new surrender charges may create.

Generally speaking, a variable annuity owner should only consider making a 1035 exchange if (1) the existing annuity is not subject to any surrender charges, and (2) the existing variable annuity is being exchanged for a new annuity that has low or no surrender charges and lower fees and expenses than the existing variable annuity. Owners of variable annuities issues prior to 1982 should consult with a tax expert prior to making a 1035 exchange due to the special tax issues associated with such annuities.

What's said: "If you're ever dissatisfied with the performance of a subaccount in your variable annuity, you can switch to another subaccount without having to pay sales loads or taxes."

<u>What's unsaid</u>: While a mutual fund investor can choose from the entire universe of mutual funds, the variable annuity owner is limited to those subaccounts that are offered within the variable annuity.

Some variable annuities offer twenty or more subaccounts, while others may offer ten or less. In some cases, the insurance company sponsoring the variable annuity may limit all, or a majority, of the available subaccounts to their proprietary products. Quite often, these proprietary products have less than stellar performance records. It should also be noted that some variable annuities do impose a fee, usually in the range of $20-25 per switch, if the variable annuity owner exceeds a certain number of subaccount switches in a year.

<u>What's said</u>: "The tax deferred growth offered by a variable annuity will allow you to pass more money on to your heirs."

<u>What's unsaid</u>: Variable annuities are terrible estate planning tools. If the variable annuity is ever annuitized, the variable annuity owner loses control of the annuity's assets and, depending on the settlement options offered and chosen, the insurance company, not the owner's heirs, may get any money remaining in the annuity when the owner dies.

If the variable annuity owner never annuitizes the annuity, then his/her heirs do receive the value of the variable annuity at the owner's death. The beneficiaries of a variable annuity must pay income tax on the portion of the proceeds that represent the capital appreciation within the annuity. Such proceeds are taxed as ordinary income instead of capital gains, generally resulting in higher taxes and significantly less money for the owner's beneficiaries.

Heirs receiving mutual funds, stocks, and ETFs as their inheritance pay no taxes due to the step-up in basis these investment products receive upon an owner's death. The value of this estate planning benefit cannot be overstated, as it allows heirs to avoid the taxes associated with variable annuities and allows the owner to accomplish their goal, to pass more of the estate to their heirs.

Fixed Indexed/Equity Indexed Annuities
Much has been written about the advantages of investing in index funds. Index funds became even more popular during the bull market of the late 80's and the 90's, as indexes regularly reported annual double-digit gains. The annuity industry quickly responded by offering an index-based annuity, commonly known as a fixed indexed, or equity indexed, annuity. While equity indexed annuities are technically fixed, rather than variable, annuities, they merit discussion due to the fact that they are tied to an equity market index.

Some might say that the marketing of equity indexed annuities can mislead the public due to the severe restrictions placed on the indexed annuity owner's ability to fully participate in an index's gain. Most equity-indexed annuities limit, or "cap," the owner's annual gain to 10 percent or less, regardless of the index's actual gain.

The owner's ability to participate in the index's gain is further restricted by the imposition of a "participation rate," typically in the range of 70-80 percent. For example, if an investor owned an equity indexed annuity that capped the annuity owner's annual gain at 10 percent, with a participation rate of 70 percent, the most that the annuity owner could earn for that year would be 7 percent (10 x .70), even if the index actually gained 30 percent that year.

Some equity-indexed annuities do offer downside protection by guaranteeing a minimum annual return, usually related to prevailing interest rates. Nevertheless, when an investor in an index based product is limited to a gain of 7 percent when the index itself shows a much larger gain, it is easy to understand why some investors may question the inherent value and fairness of the product.

Riders
Most annuities offer the owner a various additional benefits for additional fees. These benefits are offered in the form of additional contract provisions, or "riders." The number of riders is too large to allow a complete discussion here. The prospective investor should analyze each rider offered to determine the true value of the benefit, if any, being offered and the effect of the additional fees. One rider currently being offered is called an "enhanced death

benefit" (EDB). The lack of a stepped-up basis for variable annuities is often an impediment to their purchase. In an effort to counter this disadvantage, the EDB pays an additional amount of money to the heirs in an attempt to mitigate the effect of the ordinary income tax that they must pay. The value of the EDB is very questionable due to the way that it is calculated and the fact that the EDB itself is also taxable. More often than not, the variable annuity owner will determine that the benefit offered by the rider simply does not justify the added cost of the rider.

Decisions

Do variable annuities ever make sense? One situation where a variable annuity may make sense is where an investor wants tax deferred growth and they have maxed out all other tax-deferred growth options, such as 401(k)s and IRAs. Another situation where variable annuities may make sense is a situation where one's profession and/or financial situation suggest a need for asset protection and the investor resides in a state that grants annuities protection against creditors.

Even then, an investor should only consider a variable annuity with low annual fees and little or no surrender charges, such as those offered by Vanguard, T. Rowe Price and TIAA-CREF, and only invest money that they can leave invested for a long time. Prospective annuity purchaser should remember Dr. Reichenstein's findings that the typical variable annuity sold by variable annuity salesmen, with annual fees and expenses of approximately 2 percent and an annual contract fee, are always a poor investment choice.[29] Investors should also look at the number and type of subaccounts offered within the variable annuity, the performance record of each subaccount, and the annual management fee charged by the subaccounts.

What options are available to investors who already own a variable annuity and are either dissatisfied with the performance of their annuity or question whether an annuity was a suitable investment for them? The question of suitability depends on various factors such as the investor's age, investment objectives, financial needs, risk tolerance level, income, and need for liquidity. Suitability determinations are best handled by a truly objective source such as an attorney or a fee-only financial planner who has a background in annuities or securities compliance.

If a determination is made that the annuity was an unsuitable investment for the investor, the investor may choose to contact the broker and brokerage firm that sold them the annuity, as well as the insurance company that sponsors the annuity, and request that the variable annuity contract be rescinded and that their original investment be refunded in full. Given the current investigations by the NASD and the SEC into questionable annuity sales practices, the sanctions that have already been assessed in some cases, and pending legal actions involving the sale of annuities, investors with suitability questions should consider seeking a professional evaluation and objective advice regarding their situation to ensure that they are not exposing themselves to unnecessary financial losses due to unsuitable investments.

Variable annuity owners whose annuity was suitable, but who are dissatisfied with the costs and/or the performance of their annuity should consider exchanging their annuity for an annuity with lower costs, low or no surrender charges, and/or a better performance record once the surrender charge period on their present annuity expires. Annuity exchanges involving annuities that are still subject to surrender charges are generally discouraged due to the loss that would be created in having to pay the surrender charges.

Ethics and Fiduciary Issues
The marketing and sale of variable annuities continues to be a hot topic with regulators. By law, brokers are only supposed to recommend products that are suitable for an investor given their investment objectives, financial needs and overall investment profile. Investment advisors are required to put a client's interests first and only recommend actions that are in a client's best interests. Unfortunately, regulators continue to find far too many cases where the brokers and advisors have failed to honor these obligations and have engaged in predatory sales and marketing practices. In fact, annuity salesmen are sometimes taught to use such predatory tactics to induce an investor to purchase a variable annuity.[30] In one story about selling variable annuities to the elderly, salesmen were

reportedly told to treat to mislead the elderly and to treat them "like blind five-year-olds" and to "put a pitchfork in their chest."

As more and more variable annuity owners figure out the trap of annuitization, fewer variable annuity owners are annuitizing their contracts. This reduction in the annuitization rate has serious implications for the insurance industry, as it means that the amount of money that they receive from annuitized variable annuities could be significantly reduced. To prevent this loss, variable annuity owners should be alert to brokers and advisors urging more of their variable annuity clients to annuitize their variable annuities.

Given the fact that annuitization can frustrate a variable annuity owner's estate plans and that there are other options available, such as systematic withdrawals, that enable variable annuity owners to tap into their variable annuity without forfeiting control of their annuity, a recommendation to annuitize may not be in a client's best interests. In such circumstances, a recommendation to annuitize may well raise ethical questions and involve possible violations of securities laws/regulations.

Another example of the variable annuity industry's seeming indifference to the best interests of the client can be seen in stories and reports prepared or sponsored by the industry comparing investments in annuities to investments in mutual funds. Close analysis of such stories and reports usually reveal that the opinions are based on assumptions heavily favoring the annuities, such as assuming that investors will only invest in mutual funds with high fees and that the fund and/or the investor will generate substantial capital gains by heavily trading the fund/account. Without such assumptions, the chances that the variable annuity will outperform the mutual fund are greatly reduced. Inexperienced investors, however, may not be able to detect such biases.

Rarely, if ever, will you find an industry-prepared or industry-sponsored analysis comparing an investment in a variable annuity to an investment in a low cost mutual fund, particularly an index fund. The low annual fees and passive management associated with index funds virtually guarantee that the variable annuity will always lose out in such comparisons. Long-term owners of stocks and ETFs could also outperform variable annuities as well since the stocks and ETFs would not be burdened by high annual fees and annual capital gains. A failure to disclose such relevant information may also raise ethical questions, particularly if the broker or advisor has a fiduciary relationship with the client.

Such issues, combined with dubious practices such as recommending the purchase of variable annuities within qualified plans and IRAs, recommending unsuitable annuity exchanges, and "bonus" annuities, raise legitimate questions as to whether recommendations to purchase variable annuities are based on the client's best interests or the higher commissions that variable annuity sales generate. Unfortunately, NASD and SEC investigations have proven that far too often the motivating factor is the latter.

Regulators have limited resources to detect and address abusive variable annuity practices. Consequently, investors must assume greater responsibility for their investment decisions and be willing to stand up for their rights when they have been misled or have suffered financial losses due to unsuitable investment advice.

Conclusion
Variable annuities are simply not an effective investment choice for most investors due to the costs, restrictions and adverse tax aspects of the product, particularly when compared to other investment options such as mutual funds and ETFs. Variable annuities are an especially poor choice as estate planning tools, as the implications of annuitization, the lack of a stepped-up basis at the variable annuity owner's death, and the unavailability of the capital gains tax to minimize taxes may actually prevent a variable annuity owner from effectively passing on his/her estate to his/her heirs.

Variable annuities are investment products that are complex and often misunderstood. The lack of available information and the multitude of options and riders usually offered in connection with variable annuities only serve to increase the confusion. Prospective variable annuity purchasers should carefully consider both what is said and what is unsaid in sales pitches for variable annuities before deciding to invest in such products.

Investors who do decide to purchase a variable annuity should only consider those with low annual fees, low or no surrender charges, and an adequate number of quality subaccounts to allow them to realize the highest returns possible. Owners of variable annuities should use systematic withdrawals, rather than annuitization, to withdraw money from the variable annuity in order to ensure that the owner's heirs, not the insurance company, receive the value of the variable annuity upon the owner's death.

InvestSense IQ: Each 1 percent in fees and other costs reduces an investor's end-return by approximately 17 percent over a twenty year period. Variable annuities often charge an annual fee of 2-2.5 percent, with subaccount fees and rider fees extra. As a result, it is not unusual for the total charge for annual fees being 4 percent or more. With regard to investment fees and costs, YOU get what you DON'T pay for.

InvestSense IQ: If you absolutely think you need an annuity, create your own DIY annuity at a much lower cost and usually an enhanced return. You can also use the AMVR™ 3.0 to ensure that the mutual funds you choose for the investment element of your DIY annuity, if applicable, are cost-efficient and otherwise prudent.

Chapter Ten
Proactive Wealth Protection

"The business of trading in securities is one in which opportunities for dishonesty are of constant recurrence and ever present. It engages acute, active minds trained in quick apprehension, decision and action. The Congress has seen fit to regulate this business....The [securities laws are] to be enforced notwithstanding the trends to be suppressed may take on more subtle and involved forms than those in which dishonesty manifests itself in cruder and less specialized activities."

In a 1999 speech, then Chairman of the Securities and Exchange Commission Arthur Levitt warned investors that they had to become more vigilant in their dealings with investment professionals and take greater overall responsibility for protecting their financial security.[8] The wisdom of Chairman Levitt's words was proven shortly thereafter with the 2000-2002 bear market's revelation of various types of inappropriate activity on Wall Street, activity that seriously undermined the public's confidence in the investment industry.

The impact of an investment loss is the same regardless of its underlying cause. Fortunately, the risk of financial loss due to such investment myths and misconceptions can be reduced by investors becoming more proactive in managing their financial affairs.

The first paragraph, of the first chapter, of this book set out the disclosure language that the SEC proposed as a regulation for a case that the Financial Planning Association filed to force the SEC to enforce a registration rule against Merrill Lynch. As noted, the SEC lost the case and never enforced the proposed disclosure language. The disclosures in the proposed clause are still applicable and would undoubtedly help investors protect themselves. And yet, for some reason the SEC will not require stockbrokers and broker-dealers to use the language to provide investors with such valuable information.

The SEC is also currently involved in a debate over whether to require anyone that provides investment advice to the public to meet the same fiduciary standards that are required of registered investment advisers. The two key fiduciary standards required of investment advisers are

1. the fiduciary duty of loyalty, which requires a fiduciary to "discharge his duties with respect to a plan solely in the interest of the participants and beneficiaries," to always act in the best interests of a customer, with "an eye solely to the customer;"[33] and
2. the fiduciary duty of prudence, which requires a fiduciary to always act "with the same care, skill, prudence and diligence under the circumstances then prevailing that a prudent man acting in a like capacity and familiar with such matters would use" in managing a similar activity.[34]

Even if an investor's situation does not automatically legally require that the fiduciary standards apply, investors should require that their stockbroker/financial advisor agree to manage their account under such standards. The agreement between the stockbroker/financial adviser and the customer acknowledging such agreement should be in writing and signed by the customer, the stockbroker/financial adviser, and an authorized officer of their broker-dealer, e.g., firm's compliance director.

Some specific "tricks of the trade" that dishonest and unethical stockbrokers and financial advisers use are:

- "B" shares in asset management/trading accounts-since "B" shares only incur "back-end load" fees if the shares are redeemed before a certain period of time, trading in such shares may result in unnecessary fees and costs.
- "C" shares-"C" shares generally impose extremely high annual expense ratios, often as high as 1 percent. Since 1 percent is often the annual fee charged by registered investment advisers (RIAs), who have to comply with rigorous rules and regulations and demanding fiduciary duties, some stockbrokers and financial advisers will recommend "C" shares in order to collect the same fees as RIAs, while avoiding the investor protection measures required of RIAs.

- "Breakpoint" violations-most mutual funds that impose "front-end loads" on the purchase of their mutual funds allow for a reduction in such "front-end loads." The breakpoints are generally based on the amount of the investor's purchase, either individually or cumulatively over a specified time, e.g., a twelve month period. Common breakpoints are in 25 basis points (0.25) increments at each investment of $25,000 and $50,000.
- 12b-1 fees-as discussed earlier, these are fees which were originally approved to help mutual funds reduce the costs of distribution of their funds. Most mutual funds are so large that these fees are unnecessary and inequitable, as the funds can more than handle such costs. Today, these fees serve no purpose other than to provide stockbrokers with an annual "bonus" as an incentive to keep their costumers in overpriced and consistently underperforming actively managed mutual funds.
- 1035 annuity exchanges-these are generally tax-free exchanges of one variable annuity for another variable annuity. Two primary issues with 1035 exchanges are the existence of any surrender charges that will be assessed by the annuity company, and the new commissions that the annuity owner will have to pay as a result of the exchange. Bottom line: Tax free does not mean cost free.
- "Working their book"-refers to the practice of stockbrokers and financial advisers calling their clients when business is slow to suggest new purchases/reallocations in order to produce new commissions. This is a perfect time for customers to ask the "why" question.

Other proactive wealth preservation steps investors should consider include

- developing and implementing effective investment risk management strategies;
- recognizing the potential impact that investment myths and misconceptions can have on an investment portfolio and adjusting a portfolio accordingly;

- replacing blind trust in financial advisors with a healthy dose of skepticism, a willingness to question financial advice, and verifying the cost-efficiency of actively managed mutual funds with the Active Management Value Ratio™ 3.0;
- using experienced and truly objective third party experts to analyze existing or proposed investment portfolios and other financial matters;
- recognizing the inherent quality of advice issues with computer produced asset allocation and portfolio optimization plans;
- never giving a stockbroker or other financial adviser discretionary power over any investment account;
- reviewing promptly and carefully all documents received from a stockbroker, investment adviser, broker-dealer, insurance company or account custodian. Failure to promptly review such documents my impact an investor's legal rights to corrections of any errors, most notably financial recovery of any losses; and
- asking "why."

Chapter Eleven
The REAL Secret to Successful Investing

Without question, the two most common questions I get asked are "What is the secret to successful investing" and "What are the best investment books." Let's start with the last question first.

My three favorite investment books, other than this one of course, are

- "Winning the Loser's Game: Timeless Strategies for Successful Investing," by Charles Ellis. This book contains so much useful information, such as the incremental cost/incremental return metric and his whole approach to investing as a defensive process.
- "A Random Walk Down Wall Street: The Time-Tested Strategies for Successful Investing," by Burton Malkiel. Another book that promotes a simple, common sense approach to investing.
- "The Intelligent Investor," by Benjamin Graham. Considered by many to be the "father of modern investing," Graham examines investing from several viewpoints. As noted, I especially like the simplicity of his suggested model portfolio and his proactive approach to wealth management.

One interesting side note regarding Graham. One of the leading advocates of using fundamental analysis in investment analysis, Graham has recently stated that he longer advocates that approach to investing. Graham now believes that the stock market has become so efficient that he is a strong advocate of investing in index funds.

As for the secret to investing, in my opinion, it is achieving consistent and positive absolute returns. All of the topics that I have discussed in this book are what I consider to be the essential components of this approach to investing.

As I mentioned, Ellis believes that one of the secrets of successful investing is the avoidance of significant losses. The avoidance of significant losses allows investors to maximize the benefits of compounding of returns. Efficiency in portfolio construction and management, both in terms of cost and risk management, are crucial factors in achieving consistent returns. InvestSense's Active Management Value Ratio™ 3.0 metric, and our proprietary Fiduciary IQ metric, which calculates the over-all consistency of a mutual fund, are valuable tools for investors, fiduciaries and attorneys in evaluating the inherent value of a fund.

Mutual fund advertisements usually tout a fund's nominal return. As discussed earlier, a mutual fund's nominal return rarely provides a meaningful picture of a fund's performance. When a fund's performance has been less favorable, funds typically reference a fund's "relative" returns, e.g., "#1 fund in our category." A fund that is #1 in its category, but suffered a loss of 20 percent still lost 20 percent. Investors obviously do not invest to lose money. We have already discussed the issues with a broker's typical responses in such situations, "everyone lost money, it's the market." Going back to the issue of consistency of returns, losses prevent investors from receiving the maximum benefit of the compounding returns.

I always like to leave an audience with something that motivates them to take action to protect themselves. Hopefully, the Active Management Value Ratio™ 3.0 metric is something that will help improve your financial security. Two quotes from Charles Ellis always seem to leave a lasting impression on investors:

[T]he incremental fees for an actively managed mutual fund relative to its incremental returns should always be compared to the fee for a comparable index relative to its returns. When you do this, you'll quickly see that the incremental fees for active management are really, really high – on average, over 100 percent incremental returns![35]

That's right: All the value added – plus more – goes to the manager, and there's nothing left over for the investors who put up all the money and took all the risks.[36]

So we've come full circle. Only work with stockbrokers and financial advisers who are willing to commit, *in writing and signed, by both the broker/adviser and their compliance officer,* to act in a fiduciary capacity in advising you as to both product recommendations and investment strategies. Fair warning, many stockbrokers and financial advisers are going to refuse to these conditions, especially to put such a commitment in a signed writing. That should immediately raise red flags.

They will tell you that they are not legally required to commit to such conditions. Right now they may be accurate. However, it is your money, your future, your financial security, so you control the conditions for someone who wants to provide you with financial advice and/or manage your account. Your way, or the highway! Trust me; there will be someone willing to agree to your terms, to put your financial interests first, to act as your honest and trusted adviser.

Hopefully this book has provided you with some valuable and useful advice. If you take nothing else away from reading this book, remember these three quick tips:

1. You get what you DON'T pay for. Each additional 1 percent in fees and costs reduces your end return by approximately 8.5 percent over ten years and 17 percent over twenty years.
2. Amateurs focus on returns; professionals focus on risk management. Approach investing as a *defensive* process to avoid significant losses.
3. Don't confuse investment "brains" with a bull market!

Good luck!

Notes

1. Brooke Southall, "Wirehouse accounts don't match client goals," *InvestmentNews,* March 12, 2007, 12.
2. Charles Paikert, "Poll: Few Advisers are 'real' wealth managers," available on the Internet at www.investmentnews.com/article/20071029/FREE/710290324?template =printart; the John Bowen post upon which the article is based is available at www.cegworldwide.com/resource/expert-team/003-bp-john-bowen.
3. 2010 IPT Elder Investor Fraud Survey, available online at www.investorprotection.org/ learn/research/?fa=eiffeSurvey.
4. E.S. Browning, "Stocks Tarnished by 'Lost Decade'," *Wall Street Journal,* March 26, 2008, Section A, Page 1
5. Charles D. Ellis, *"Investment Policy: How To Win the Loser's Game,"* 2nd Ed., (Chicago, IL: Irwin Professional Publishing, 1993), 49
6. Harry M. Markowitz, *Portfolio Selection*, 2nd Ed. (Cambridge, MA: Basil Blackwood & Sons, Inc., 1991), 6-7
7. Richard O. Michaud, *Efficient Asset Management: A Practical Guide to Stock Portfolio Optimization and Asset Allocation* (Boston, MA: Harvard Business School Press, 1998), 36
8. Gary P. Brinson, L. Randolph Hood and Gilbert L. Beebower, "Determinants of Portfolio Performance," *Financial Analysts Journal* 42 (July/August 1986): 39-4
9. Brinson, et al., 39
10. William S. Sharpe, *Investors and Markets: Portfolio Choices, Asset Prices and Investment Advice* (Princeton, NJ: Princeton University Press, 2006), 206-209
11. Charles D. Ellis, *"Investment Policy: How To Win the Loser's Game,"* 2nd Ed., (Chicago, IL: Irwin Professional Publishing, 1993), Ellis – defensive process
12. Benjamin Graham, *The Intelligent Investor: The Definitive Book on Value Investing,"* (New York, NY; Harper Business Essentials, 2003)
13. Harry M. Markowitz, *Portfolio Selection*, 2nd Ed. (Cambridge, MA: Basil Blackwood & Sons, Inc., 1991), 6-7
14. Charles D. Ellis, *"Winning the Loser's Game: Timeless Strategies for Successful Investing,"* 6th Ed., (New York, NY, 2018),

52, 98

15. Benjamin Graham, *The Intelligent Investor: The Definitive Book on Value Investing,"* (New York, NY; Harper Business Essentials, 2003)

16. <u>Tibble v. Edison International</u>, 135 S. Ct. 1823, 1828 (2015).

17. Restatement Third, Trusts § 90 (The Prudent Investor Rule), comment e(1), copyright 2007 by The American Law Institute. All excerpts from the Restatement herein are reprinted with permission. All rights reserved. Restatement 90 b

18. Restatement Third, Trusts § 90 (The Prudent Investor Rule), comment e(1), copyright 2007 by The American Law Institute. All excerpts from the Restatement herein are reprinted with permission. All rights reserved. Restatement 90 f

19. Restatement Third, Trusts § 90 (The Prudent Investor Rule), comment e(1), copyright 2007 by The American Law Institute. All excerpts from the Restatement herein are reprinted with permission. All rights reserved. Restatement 90 h(2)

20. Charles D. Ellis, "The End of Active Investing," *Financial Times*, January 20, 2017 https://www.ft.com/content/6b2d5490-d9bb-11e6-944b-e7eb37a6aa8e.

21. Charles D. Ellis, *"Winning the Loser's Game: Timeless Strategies for Successful Investing,"* 6th Ed., (New York, NY, 2018, 10.

22. Burton Malkiel, *"A Random Walk Down Wall Street,"* 11th Ed., (W.W. Norton & Co., 2016), 460.

23. Philipp Meyer-Brauns, "Mutual Fund Performance Through a Five-Factor Lens," Dimensional Funds Advisers, L.P., August 2016.

24. Ross Miller, "Measuring the True Cost of Active Management by Mutual Funds," *Journal of Investment Management,* Vol. 5, No. 1 (2007), 22, 29-49.

25. http://www.investsense.com

26. W. Reichenstein, "Who Should Buy A Nonqualified Tax-Deferred Annuity," Financial Services Review, Vol. 11, No. 1, (Spring 2002), p.30. (with permission)

27. Reichenstein, p.30

28. Moshe Milevsky and Steven Posner, "The Titanic Option: Valuation of the Guaranteed Death Benefit in Variable Annuities and Mutual Funds," *Journal of Risk and Insurance,* Vol. 68, No. 1, (2001), 91-126.

29. J. Opdyke, Shifting Annuities May Help Brokers More Than Investors, Wall St. J., Feb. 16, 2001, at C1.
30. Arthur Levitt, "Common Sense Investing in the 21st Century Marketplace," *www.sec.gov/ news/speech/speecharchive/1999/ spch324.htm*
31. E. Schultz and J. Opdyke, Annuities 101: How to Sell to Senior Citizens, Wall St. J., July 2, 2002, at C1
32. Archer quote this is correct from 803 in opinion
33. Restatement Third, Trusts § 90 (The Prudent Investor Rule), comment e(1), copyright 2007 by The American Law Institute. All excerpts from the Restatement herein are reprinted with permission. All rights reserved. Restatement 77 ? loyalty
34 Restatement Third, Trusts § 90 (The Prudent Investor Rule), comment e(1), copyright 2007 by The American Law Institute. All excerpts from the Restatement herein are reprinted with permission. All rights reserved. Restatement 78 pru?
Rest 78 pru
35. Charles Ellis, "My Investment Letter: Words of Advice for My Grandchildren," AAII Journal, October 2013, PAGE
36. Charles Ellis, "Winning the Loser's Game," 6th ed., (New York, NY/McGraw-Hill 2018), 164.

Recommended Reading

"The 60-Second Investor Protection Kit," available online at https://www.linkedin.com/pulse/60-second-investor-protection-kit-james-watkins-iii-jd-cfp-/

C.T. Geer, "The Great Annuity Rip-off," Forbes, February 9, 1998.

J. Kalter, "Annuities: Just Say No," Worth, July/August 1996.

National Association of Security Dealers, "NASD Investor Alert: Should You Exchange Your Variable Annuity?," February 15, 2001, available on the Internet at www.nasdr.com/alert_02_01.htm.

About the Author

James W. Watkins, III, J.D., CFP®, AWMA® is a 1977 honors graduate of Georgia State University and a 1981 graduate of Notre Dame Law School. He has been a member of the State Bar of Georgia since 1981. He is the owner of The Watkins Law Firm.

Mr. Watkins is the Founder and CEO/Managing Member of InvestSense, LLC, an investment education firm that provides fiduciary prudence oversight services, quality of investment advice analyses, wealth management programs and forensic risk management analyses to individuals, pension plans, educational institutions and other groups, including strategies for fiduciary risk management and wealth preservation.

He is both a CERTIFIED FINANCIAL PLANNER™ professional and an Accredited Wealth Management Advisor^{SM}. He is also a CFP® Ambassador. He has extensive experience in the areas of fiduciary prudence oversight, quality of investment advice analysis, fiduciary law, financial planning, asset protection/wealth preservation, securities/ ERISA law and estate planning.

Mr. Watkins is the owner of two blogs - "CommonSense InvestSense" (investsense.com), an investor protection blog for investors, and "The Prudent Fiduciary Rules" (iainsight.wordpress.com), a "best practices" blog for investment advisers and other investment professionals.

Mr. Watkins has written numerous articles on the subject of investing, wealth management and preservation, asset protection, and 401(k)/pension law. His work has appeared on, and he has been quoted or referenced on sites such as the Atlanta Journal-Constitution, the Washington Post, USAToday.com, Fox Business.com, Huffington Post, the "Money Savage" podcast, The Evidence Based Investor (TEBI), financialplanning.com, and the institutionalinvestor.com.

He is the author of three books, available at amazon.com and barnesandnoble.com

S. Burns, "Why Variable Annuities Are No Match For Index Funds," available on the Internet at moneycentral.msn.com

- "CommonSense InvestSense: New Strategies for Accumulating and Preserving Wealth"
- "The Prudent Investment Adviser Rule: Risk and Liability Management for Investment Fiduciaries"
- "The 401(k)/403(b) Investment Manual: What Plan Participants and Plan Sponsors REALLY Need to Know"

He is also the author of the law review article, "Modern Portfolio Theory, the Prudent Investor Rule and Fiduciary Investing" (PIABA Law Review), available online at https://iainsight.wordpress.com/mpt-the-prudent-investor-rule-and-fiduciary-investing/

You can follow Mr. Watkins online at

- LinkedIn - jw3investsensellc
- Twitter – @investsense

You can contact Mr. Watkins by email at
- investsensellc@gmail.com
- jwat3@yahoo.com

www.ingramcontent.com/pod-product-compliance
Lightning Source LLC
Chambersburg PA
CBHW051331220526
45468CB00004B/1586